Advance Praise for *My Mother's Daughter*

"What a fascinating, inspiring and enjoyable read about the incredible life adventures and impact of my wonderful friend, Chief Mrs Taiwo Taiwo, an unstoppable force, passionate and driven to deliver change, and help others in Nigeria, especially in her hometown of Lagos. This is a manual for what it takesto be an activist over a lifetime! And a clarion call to never, ever give up. It is ariveting read from a fresh perspective and honest voice."

— PAMELA WATSON, author of *Gibbous Moon Over Lagos: Pursuing a Dreamon Africa's Wild Side*, formerly Australia's Honorary Consul to Lagos and the eighteen southern states of the Nigerian Federation, corporate advisor, explorer and entrepreneur

"This is a marvelous and outstanding book written in Taiwo's usual conversationaland brilliant style only one who writes as well as she could possibly have written. It's a great piece of work that chronicles her amazing, versatile life as a property developer, philanthropist, educationalist, and social entrepreneur.

My Mother's Daughter telegraphs how her work is inspired by her mantra in life,'living for good to do good,' and continues to propel her to new and greater heights and accomplishments. Her effervescent and vivacious personality comesthrough in the book as it is in every facet of her life, and makes her a truly wonderful personality from whom one never ceases to learn and enjoy. One theme that comes across so well in the book is a reflection of a quote from Mahatma Gandhi, 'be the change you wish to see in the world.' Taiwo's life vividly demonstrates this principle by being that change she wishes to see in theworld.

I resoundingly recommend this fascinating debut about living for others and thereward of hard work, deep faith, and selfless living. It is really a great, riveting piece of work."

— DR STELLA OKOLI (OON), CEO/MD, Emzor Pharmaceutical Industries

"I was once asked to review a book, and after reading the book, the first term that came to mind was 'unputdownable'. I checked a few online dictionaries, and voila, the term was already listed as a modern English word. So when I picked this book, *My Mother's Daughter*, and started to read, and I discovered thatI could not drop the book until I had finished it, I said to myself, this is another*unputdownable* book.

My Mother's Daughter shows that we should all be activists because our society offers several areas where urgent change is needed. Chief Taiwo has shown thateveryone can make a change if we really want to. I will recommend this book toanyone who is interested in making a change."

— TUNJI ADEYINKA, GMD, The Republicom Group

"Described by Taiwo as her mother's story, *My Mother's Daughter* is really Taiwo's autobiographical description of how her life has been a reflection of the forceful personality of the uniquely Nigerian, Ijebu woman who was her mother. This—the telling of an atypical mother-daughter 'mentoring' relationship—is what sets the backdrop for the book and makes it engrossing for international and Nigerian readers alike.

My Mother's Daughter is not just a lively, captivating account of the birth and nurturing of Taiwo's strong personality, which she unabashedly owns, it is a racy introduction for newbies into Nigerian culture and Yoruba family life; it is alsoa nostalgic read for older Nigerians, with choice bits of Taiwo's recollections ofsocial and political events offering engaging material for reflection and discussion. Younger Nigerians, particularly women, will be inspired by this example of a 'can-do' spirit as they delve into the stories behind these truly commendable successes. Taiwo's ability to keep us riveted in a conversation about her action-filled life story will keep you reading till the very end. *My Mother's Daughter* doesnot disappoint!"

— DR MODUPE IRELE, Ambassador of the Federal Republic of Nigeria to France

"*My Mother's Daughter*. A tour de force of achievement in business, in private life,and in community. Written with flourish, I hear my Sis Taiwo telling the story,filling in the blanks of the years before we met with a conversational, engagingstyle, humorous wide-eyed innocent mischievousness, and an unapologeticsincerity.

In *My Mother's Daughter*, we are given a history of contemporary Nigeria—especially Lagos—through the life of our protagonist. There are lessons to be learnt from the entrepreneur who did it afraid, scaling hurdles of sexism, the government changing goal posts, corporate Nigeria reneging on its agreements,and Chief (Mrs) Taiwo Taiwo never giving up in spite of jealousy from variousrelationships. The most important lesson however, is that all great achievementsare made possible with hard committed work and the right team. *My Mother's Daughter*, a must read for all who want impact through generations."

— JOKE SILVA, Co-founder, the Lufodo Group

Fascinating read...
I Did not want it to end so found myself deliberately slowing down the read.

All sorts of emotions running through my mind, as I read this fascinating riveting book Reading the part about furnishing the apartment in London... audacious in the extreme... After reading the last line on the page 108. "it was gratifying to know how proud she was of me". Of course she was, and anyone who cannot recognise that, ...Eat your heart out... go write your own book if you have anything you're proud of.... Chief Mrs is a Trail Blazer jor... End of discussion!

MR. AKIN OSINBAJO (SAN), Senior Partner Abdulai Taiwo & Co

"An unputdownable book"
Highly recommended book, history laden, cultural and educative,

Do you know the whole 50 acres of land making up Shonibare Estate was purchased at £5,000?

How the 1st TV station in Africa was sealed, schooling in England as a black person in the early 60's etc.

Written by a timeless woman of grace.
Chief Taiwo Taiwo

MR. YEMI EDUN, Managing Director- Daniel Fords- Leading Property Consultant

Some parts of the book touched me so very much. I was especially moved reading about Abioye and her tragic death, but amazed by what you have done with the foundation. Your tremendous efforts in pulling through so many projects, including the Ajele fire station can only be rewarded by the Almighty. Sadly, in Nigeria, National honours and recognition are rarely bestowed to those who merit Nigeria does not give honour to those that deserve it, sadly and most unfortunately to our failed Political class. Who needs their rewards anyway.

I learnt so many things I did not know about you and your family after reading the book. We give glory to God for your life and achievements. The book should encourage the youths of today that with hard work, dedication and commitment, you can still achieve a lot in Nigeria. God will continue to protect you and your family, grant you more wisdom, strength, good health and long life in Jesus mighty name.

MR. SEGUN OLAYE MD/CEO- Ayoola Foods

In My Mother's Daughter, Taiwo Taiwo argues that mentoring the next generation is important for any true transformation to take place in our country. And to bring about any positive change, she says that agonizing alone will not solve the country's seemingly intractable problems. So, she encourages people to organize, organize, and organize again around causes that will make our world a better place to live in. If the goal of Taiwo Taiwo is to deliver a book that is compassionate and inspiring, she brilliantly achieves it, with My Mother's Daughter.

MR KUNLE AJIBADE, Executive Editor/Director of The NEWS/PM NEWS, is the author of Jailed for Life: A Reporter's Prison Notes and What A Country!

ISBN: 978-978-58494-5-5

Published in Nigeria in 2021 by Quramo Publishing,
under its QBooks imprint.

The Simi Johnson Centre
13 Sinari Daranijo Street, Victoria Island,
Lagos, Nigeria.
+234 01 454 7878
info@quramo.com
www.quramo.com

Cover Illustration and Design by: Ayebabeledaipre Sokari.

A catalogue record of this book will be available from the National Library of Nigeria.

My Mother's Daughter

TAIWO TAIWO

To the memory of Chief Mrs Alice Olaperi Shonibare,

My Mother, My Icon, My Anchor, My Pillar, My Strength.

Thank you for loving me so much, and for teaching me how to love.

Contents

Foreword

I recall a telephone discussion with Chief Taiwo Taiwo early in 2020 when we were faced with the certainty of a lockdown, a fallout of the COVID-19 pandemic. She informed me she would use the opportunity to conclude the book she was writing, a work of non-fiction dealing with her life experiences. This relatively brief dialogue revealed several thingsto me; here was a woman who was not about to waste a period during which she would be compelled to stay indoors. She was persuaded that some of her life experiences were worth sharing, and she had already begun the process of chronicling them. I have seen my cousin's tenacityof purpose and keen sense of focus upfront and personal in the way and manner in which she approached the collaboration between Carleton University in Canada and Atlantic Hall School of which she is Chairmanof the Board of Governors.

It is not surprising that her book would be inspired by her belovedlate mother, Chief Mrs Alice Olaperi Shonibare, a towering figure and an iconic personality in business circles and in society. She was my dad's 'sista' (pronounced with a distinctive Yoruba tone). In actual fact, they were cousins; my father's mother and Chief Mrs Shonibare's father were the siblings (Olukoyas), children of Oremadegun, the Oba (traditional ruler) of Odogbolu (a town in South Western Nigeria). In Nigeria, it is not out of place to call a cousin 'sista' or 'broda'. My dad and Chief Mrs Shonibare had a close relationship, and I have very fond memories of her. My mother told me of visits she paid to the Shonibare residence at

Kensington, London, in the 1960s, and the lavish hospitality she enjoyed.I recall with fondness my first encounter with her when my mother andI came back from the UK in 1965, and we visited her at her impressive residence in Maryland Estate, Ikeja. My aunt was present and significantly involved in my wedding ceremonies. She supported me during the burial ceremonies of both of my parents who died within three years of each other in the 1990s. She was particularly fond of my mum who like herself was an Ile-Ife chief, courtesy of Oba Okunade Sijuwade.

As one finds out from reading the book, my aunt became a widowat forty-one and went on to raise eight children while taking the family business to dizzying heights, building on what her husband left behind, and inspiring this riveting piece of non-fiction. My experience with her was personal, and I recall the warmth, the favour and the generosity, she bestowed on me.

My Mother's Daughter illustrates a number of themes and values I have come to espouse over the years. They may not amount to fresh revelation to many readers, but what I find instructive is that Chief Taiwo has lived these values in a tangible manner. The book affirms that you only really fail in life when you never attempt to achieve your goals. Also, if we utilise a fraction of the potential we have as individuals, we wouldbe quite surprised at the outcome, and the world would probably be an entirely different place.

Chief Mrs Taiwo's life experiences teach us what I consider a very important theme that runs through *My Mother's Daughter*: it is an exercise in futility to keep complaining about the way things are if we are not willing to do something about it. In Nigeria, we have many armchair critics who have made a career of pontificating on the issues of the day but have not done a whole lot to improve the state of affairs. Chief Taiwomade it a habit to attempt to change things she felt could have been better. Not getting the result we are looking for does not mean we shouldnot keep trying.

The last lesson I would like to draw attention to is that when we allow Him, God is able to bring life out of death. From the depths of pain occasioned by the loss of a precious daughter, the author created a number of positive initiatives under the Aart of Life Foundation. These served to keep 'Bioye's memory alive, and continue to benefit people who are in need.

The value of our lives will be measured by the impact we have on others. This point of view leads us to acknowledge that the author in under seventy years, has lived a life worthy of emulation and celebration,and *My Mother's Daughter* is evidence of that fact…but if I know my 'big sis' well enough, she is not done yet! Expect more.

I recommend this book strongly. Once you start reading, you mayfind it hard to put it down until you finish. It is captivating, enlightening,and highly informative.

Ambassador Adeyinka Olatokunbo Asekun
Nigeria's High Commissioner to Canada

Preface

I always knew I had to write my mother's story. I simply had to. So profound was her impact on almost every aspect of my life. She was a tremendous, rare phenomenon, an attribute underscored by the fact that she was self-effacing, humble, and respectful.

My mother was fearless, with a single-minded determination that sometimes made me nervous, and terribly worried for her! Above all, she had one of the most intuitive, forward-looking business minds I would ever encounter in my life.

One would never imagine she had such a rarefied pedigree, the eldest child of Chief Samuel Ademola Olukoya, the first African manager of the United Africa Company (UAC). UAC was the successor of The Royal Niger Company, which was chartered by the British Governmentin the 19th century. The Royal Niger Company existed for a short time before making its overt intention clear by renaming it the United Africa Company (UAC), which came under the control of Unilever in the 1930s.

The Royal Niger Company was instrumental in the formationof Colonial Nigeria as it enabled the British Empire to establish control over the lower Niger against the German competition led by Bismarck during the 1890s. In 1900, the company-controlled territories became the Southern Nigerian Protectorate, which was united with the Northern Nigerian Protectorate to form the colony and protectorate of Nigeria in 1914.

History is unambiguous; the colonisation of Nigeria by the Britishwas purely a matter of self-interest, with the sole aim of protecting their vested businesses which had been established by the United AfricaCompany. In effect, this company owned Nigeria.

Her father, Chief Samuel Ademola Olukoya, having been well-tutored by UAC, resigned with the full blessing of his former employers to become a produce buyer and merchant across the western states of Nigeria and beyond. In the process, he became an extremely wealthy businessman. It must be acknowledged that the smart Africans who were selected to work in UAC, a behemoth of an intercontinental organisation, and who went through their rigorous, robust and comprehensive tutelage which in today's world could be compared to having undergone an MBA in Harvard, were the best business minds around.

My Mother's Daughter started as a homage to my mother; I had this compelling need to tell her story. As I proceeded, it became clear in so doing, that so very much of my life was inextricably linked to her. I could not have achieved, or even dared attempt to embark on so many of the gutsy initiatives I took on in my life, if I had not had such a formidable role model as my mother.

In telling my story, *My Mother's Daughter,* I discovered she had led me on my journey to becoming who I am, who I could be. This book is dedicated to my darling mother, Chief Mrs Alice Olaperi Shonibare. I can never honour her enough for loving me so much, and in the process, teaching me how to love.

Taiwo Taiwo

MY MOTHER'S DAUGHTER

I never really understood why it was that Mummy concluded, and soearly too, that she wanted me to work in the family business. God knows that was not my choice of a career path. She was fond ofrecalling a series of incidents that occurred when I was a young child. I could not have been more than eight years old.

My mother was equally invested, along with my father, in their flagship company, Shonny Investments and Properties Company Limited, and its various subsidiaries; she was well-informed and aware of the minutest details of his myriad business interests. They were undoubtedlya formidable team, both intuitive and forward-looking entrepreneurs.

She nevertheless took a backseat in the direct management of the company. Instead, she immersed herself in trading. I think it wasan instinctive Ijebu thing, and my mum was the quintessential Ijebu woman. I cannot remember a time when she was not involved in one sort of trading or the other; no matter that she was married to one of the most successful entrepreneurs of her generation, with whom she had a dynamic business partnership.

She had a petrol station right in front of our childhood home, for goodness' sake, with cars queuing up daily to fill up their tanks. She also sold cooking gas and kerosene, but like the true Ijebu lady she was, her true passion was trading in *aso-oke*, the traditional woven fabric used by Yoruba people as 'uniforms' for friends and family during special events. Every occasion was an excuse to party: funerals, naming ceremonies, weddings, the list goes on. It is not without reason that the Yorubas are described in the *Encyclopaedia Britannica* as "the fun-loving, party-giving tribe of West Africa". She truly enjoyed the creativity involved in designing, mixing, and matching colours of the handwoven fabric.

A downside of trading in this manner, which often involved selling on credit to friends and family, was the perennial problem of collecting your money from debtors, who were, invariably, family and friends, manyof whom frankly thought she did not need to be paid and could jolly well afford to subsidise their lifestyles.

Mummy, ever the shrewd but self-effacing businesswoman she undoubtedly was, decided she would unleash her special 'weapons' to chase her recalcitrant debtors and somehow embarrass them to pay up.

The twins, Kehinde, my twin sister, and I, were these weapons, sent separately by my mother with a simple mission: Mama Kwara, Aunty Abiola, Mama Funmi—or some other aunty—is owing her this much for fabrics supplied, and it is long overdue; *don't come back empty-handed.*

She recounted the story often: "Taiwo never came back without collecting the debt in full."

I would simply sit at the debtor's home all day, and persistently, albeit politely, inform her, "Aunty, my mummy sent me to collect the money owed for the *aso-oke.*" Typically, these debtors were months andmonths behind the agreed credit limit.

I would be ignored, which was easy to do since I was just a little eight-year-old girl, but I would hold my own and simply sit it out.

"Mummy says I must not come home until I have collected the money, Ma," I would say respectfully.

A few hours later, the lady would pass by me still sitting patientlyin her living room.

"What is wrong with this child?" she would bellow.

I would reply again, very meekly, "Mummy says I must not come home, Ma, without the money."

Utterly frustrated and irritated, she would reluctantly give in, handing over what she owed my mother, in full.

"Thank you, Ma," I would say, and rush home victorious, eager togive the money to my mum.

"Thank you, my husband," was my mum's typical response. 'My husband' was the endearment she used for her children, whenever she was particularly pleased with any of us.

My twin sister, Kehinde, never had such luck; perhaps she didn't have my tenacity, or simply believed the fibs told by these perennial debtors.

"Mummy," she would say, returning empty-handed, "They don't have the money."

So it was that my mother, as she tells it, always knew I had the requisite gravitas to be part of the family business.

EARLY YEARS IN LAGOS

My siblings and I were enrolled in different schools all across Lagos, in pairs of two. We were all roughly two years apart in age, almost to the day. The two eldest, Ronke and Yinka, attended Anglican Girls Primary School on Lagos Island, while my twin sister and I attended Reagan Memorial Baptist Nursery and Primary School in Yaba. We lived in our childhood home at Number 1, Spencer Street, Yaba, Lagos.

My parents tell a hilarious tale of my first couple of days at school.I evidently believed that school was simply an avenue to meet and play with new friends. On my third day, I went up to the class teacher and declared, "I want to go home now!"

She replied something to the effect of, *Are you kidding me?* Not the least bit perturbed, I repeated, "I want to go home now. I have spent three days playing with you, and it is becoming boring!"

She laughed and explained that this was a school, a place to learn,and not simply a playground. That was my attitude to school workat that time; not surprisingly with that attitude, I was asked to repeat Nursery One, whilst my twin sister moved on to Nursery Two. But being extremely close, truly the best of friends, we naturally always hung outtogether during school breaks.

The headmistress of the school at the time was Mrs Harrison, whoI remembered to be mean, and dare I say, quite sadistic.

One fine day, my sister and I were playing together during break time, as we always did. Mrs Harrison came up to me and bellowed, "What are you doing spending break time with your twin sister? Don't you know you are in Class 1, and she's in Class 2, you dunce? Your break time is over. Go back to your class!" ending her rebuke with a few morechoice words.

I went back to my class as instructed, sad and crushed by the onslaught of harsh words from this authority figure who was supposed to be nurturing me and fostering an atmosphere in school where I could thrive as a pupil.

The next day, she stopped me in my tracks just as I was about to walk into my classroom.

"You cannot go in!" she said. "You must stay outside of the classas punishment. That is the problem with you children with rich parents; you think you can do whatever you like! Well, I can tell you right now, your rich daddy can take you to school anywhere in the world, but itwill never make a difference; a dunce you are and a dunce you always will be." As a child, I couldn't understand this vendetta she had against me, but it is clear as day now that she was hell-bent on putting me in myplace, not because I had done anything wrong, but because of who I wasand my family's socioeconomic background. It was a cruel way to treat a child.

After spending an hour outside of my class, watching everyone else inside as they carried on with the day's lesson, I decided I might as well head home. I must have been about eight years old at the time.

We had moved from our childhood home on Spencer Street, Yaba, which was close to Reagan Memorial Baptist School, to MarylandEstate, a private estate, the first of its kind in Lagos, built by my parents' company, Shonny Investments and Properties Co. Ltd. The estate was my father's long-held vision and ambition finally realised. We had moved to our new home on the estate, the Grecian-inspired Maryland Villa.

It was off Airport Road and a good ten kilometres away from school.

I honestly do not recall having the faintest of fears or nerves in methat day. It was simply an act of defiance, a deliberate one, to remove myself from where I evidently was not wanted.

I left the school—no one noticed me walking out of the school gate—and started my long walk home to Maryland, on the busy IkoroduRoad.

I derived so much pleasure from observing everything around me,so I was probably engrossed in absorbing every detail as I made my waydown Ikorodu Road.

It did occur to me that if I became really tired, my father's older brother, whom we called Papa Ibadan, had a house on that Road, and I could always stop there.

As fate would have it, I had barely gotten on the busy Ikorodu Road when the driver who did our school runs spotted me as he headed back to the house, having done his daily school drop-off, starting at Reagan, Yaba, continuing to drop Yinka off at Anglican School in Lagos Island, and finally, Ronke, who attended Holy Child College in Obalende, the Catholic secondary school where students wore the unique cherubic school uniform.

He stopped dead in his tracks when he saw me, all by myself, walking on such a major road.

"What on earth are you doing out of school? Your parents are going to be very upset with you."

His words suddenly made me apprehensive; I dreaded my parents' reaction when they discovered what I had done. *What was I thinking?*

When I arrived home, in a flood of tears, I was taken aback by my parents' reaction. Their first thought was, "How on earth were you able to simply walk out of school without anyone noticing? No one noticed? What if you had been kidnapped, or worse?"

I dramatically recounted my story, having always had a flair for being over the top! My father was enraged, absolutely furious, particularly at the insidious cruelty of the headmistress to a young child.

He took me straight back to school, asked me to pack my belongings, headed to Kehinde's class, and had her pack all her stuff too. He had a few choice words for the headmistress, who was, by now, really perturbed; he promised to feature her in an article on abuse of children at schools the very next day in his widely read newspaper, *The Daily Express*.

We left Reagan Memorial Baptist School in the most dramatic manner imaginable, never to come back, never to see some of our childhood friends again.

Not long after this incident, my parents decided all eight of us children—six girls and two boys—must be educated in England.

MY BELOVED PARENTS

My father, Chief Samuel Olatunbosun Shonibare, was an astutebusinessman, widely recognised as being well ahead of his time. He'd acquired fifty acres of land on what later became Airport Road, from the Onigbongbo family in 1955. He rightly predictedthat its proximity to the proposed airport would make it a gold mine, andacquired it for five thousand pounds (£5,000).

Many thought he was mad because at the time, the area was a mere village. Of course later, he was proven to be prescient in making this investment. Throughout his career, he would repeatedly demonstratethis instinct for making winning business deals.

The land was acquired under the name of Chief S.O. Shonibare, but in 1959, as part of the conditions of the £250,000 loan he received from Barclays Bank DCO to execute the project, he changed the name on the title deeds to a new company he'd formed that year—Shonny Investments and Properties Limited—and built what is now called the Shonibare Estate. Back then, it was called Maryland Estate, arguably thefirst mixed residential estate in Nigeria.

The estate comprised thirteen bungalows, eight blocks of fully furnished two-bedroom flats, and later, six duplexes. It boasted special features like a borehole and gas lamps fitted in the sitting rooms, which was quite impressive considering, at that time, the country had no water and electricity problems like we have now. Plans were underway to provide the estate with standby generators in the 1960s when electricity was in more than adequate supply for Lagos's population of 763,000 people.

He foresaw the explosion of the population, as well as rapid industrialisation and urbanisation. He so accurately gauged the fact that the infrastructure in place would simply not be able to keep up with the rapid expansion of the industrial base of Nigeria. How very right he was!

Nigeria currently generates 4,600 megawatts nationwide againsta national electricity demand of 160,000 megawatts! Contrast this with South Africa's generating capacity of 250,000 megawatts. The shortfall is staggering and why a good portion of the country's population is dependent on standby generators. It also underscores how much of a visionary my father, Chief Shonibare, truly was.

Before his death at the age of forty-four, he'd already begun holding discussions with international organisations such as Sony and Woolworths, to partner in various business ventures. His great mentor and anchor was Lord Roy Thomson of Fleet Street, who led the joint venture with Action Group, the political group established by Chief Awolowo, to create *The Amalgamated Press*, of which *The Daily Express* was one of the most popular in its staple.

Lord Thomson was a Canadian who became the quintessential Englishman; a media magnate with a media empire, which at a point in time included more than two hundred newspapers in Canada, the United States, the United Kingdom, and Nigeria. Lord Thomson wasthe owner of a diverse group of companies with interests in publishing, printing, television, and travel. He joined J. Paul Getty, the British petrol-industrialist and patriarch of the Getty family, in a consortium that successfully explored for oil in the North Sea. Lord Thomson was also the first Baron of Fleet Street, and was the last person to be given a hereditary peerage into the British House of Lords. He was the critical link, through our father, that helped the Western Nigerian government set up a television station over 60 years ago, the first in Africa and one of the first anywhere in the world.

Lord Thomson took Chief Shonibare as his adopted son. He was a huge part of our family. And when complications from my father's excessive high blood pressure led to kidney disease and claimed his life on 17 January 1964, in London, Lord Thomson together with my mother, were the only two by his bedside at the University College Hospital.

He remained close to my mother and our family till his death, andhis son and heir, Lord Kenneth, never failed to send us Christmas cards.His father had impressed upon him that he should forever consider the Shonibares family.

MY BELOVED PARENTS

My parents had eight children; by the time they had their fifth daughter,Idowu, they—especially my mother—were becoming desperate to havea son.

Kehinde and I, the twins, were the third and fourth, right bangin the middle of a large family. In Yoruba culture, twins are considered special gifts from God, good luck charms, and are to be treated as such. For this reason, my parents were called Mama and Papa Ronke, after the eldest child, Ronke, but were equally likely to be referred to as Mama and Papa *Ibeji*[1].

My parents were extremely loving and supportive. Kehinde and I,as one would expect being twins, were very close; we created and existedin our own little bubble within the family, which must have made our immediate younger sister feel particularly left out. It probably didn't help that her birthday was on 15 February, just a day before ours on the 16th. She was more likely than not, poor thing, obliged to wait a day and celebrate her birthday with us on the 16th.

Then there was my grandmother, my father's mother; he simply revered the steps she walked on, the air she breathed. We called her *Iya Agba*[2], although, come to think of it, why on earth should we have called such a beautiful young lady, *Iya Agba*?

She absolutely adored Kehinde and I, and very unusually, shehad a very loving relationship with my mother, her daughter-in-law, who equally loved her to bits. My mother took her as the mother she'd lost when she was only thirteen, a heart-breaking loss for her. *Iya Agba* provided the maternal love and support she'd been missing.

She lived in Ijebu Ode, my father's hometown, but would visit usin Lagos; we were all thrilled whenever we knew she was coming. She particularly loved having Kehinde and I over to stay with her in Ijebu Ode, which relieved my mother from the hard work of raising young children so close in age.

I suspect she also loved showing off her twins; being the grandmaof twins was a badge of honour. She would spoil us rotten during our stay with her, and would take us everywhere.

Tall, slim, elegant, and stunningly beautiful, she resembled aFulani—the large ethnic group dispersed across West Africa—withdistinct, fine features.

She was a devout Muslim. Kehinde and I spent one unforgettable Sallah holiday with her in Ijebu Ode. She took us everywhere to experience the feasts and the general revelry that characterise Sallah celebrations. As we went from place to place, I observed everything around me, and my imagination wandered off into another world. Before I knew it, I got lost in the milling crowd.

I honestly do not remember feeling apprehensive about getting separated from my grandma and Kehinde; so utterly engrossed I was by the spectacle all around me.

1. *Mother and father of twins*
2. *Old Mama*

I learnt later that my grandma was beside herself, looking for me everywhere, in sheer terror and panic. She went home with Kehinde, letting everyone know that her granddaughter, Taiwo, was missing! Her cries of terror must have reverberated around the entire town. Mama's twin is lost!

Still engrossed in whatever it was that had so absorbed my attention,I was oblivious to the panic I had created. Suddenly, a lady passed by me and screamed, "Taiwo!" jolting me out of my thoughts.

"Yes, Ma," was my response, still unaware of all the commotion I'd caused. It wasn't long before the whole town found out, relieved, that Mama Agba's twin granddaughter had been found.

The kind lady took me straight home. I'll never forget my grandma continuously screeching, "Yeh pa! I have lost Laperi's daughter! Yeh! Oh,I am undone. How will I ever explain this to her?!"

She sent us packing the very next day, back to our parents! Who could blame her?

I loved *Iya Agba* very much, but sadly she died young, sometime in her late 40s, due to complications from breast cancer, a disease which was quite rarely diagnosed in those days. It was my first experience of losinga loved one. My father was inconsolable, as was the entire household. Those were sad, dark days.

My family lived on 1 Spencer Street, Yaba, the same house where I wasborn. The house was provided by UAC where my father worked as an executive at the time.

Our next-door neighbours were the Abebes, also UAC senior managers. They had seven children, all born, like us, two years apart. Kehinde and I were particularly close to John, who later became Dr John Abebe.

It was a happy childhood, with lots of comings and goings. My father was also a politician, one of the seven founders of the Action Group, the political party that fought hard for Nigeria's independence with its formidable leader and visionary, Chief Awolowo, who was simply called 'Leader' by all.

My father, the financial brain of the party, was also known for his writing prowess. Politics was the enduring conversation in our household, and I grew up extremely inquisitive about all things related to it and to world affairs.

At five years old, I knew everything about the remarkable life of Mahatma Gandhi. I was fascinated by it all. Prone, as I undoubtedly was, to get lost in my imagination, my mind wandered far and wide to marvel at all the amazing, pivotal events taking place in the world, particularly the fight for independence, in various countries all over the world, fromthe British Empire.

I remember how flabbergasted my teachers were at my first schoolin England, that I could rattle off the names of the Secretary-General of the United Nations, U. Thant; the President of the United States, John F. Kennedy; and that I knew the names of most capitals of the world. They found it bizarre that someone so young could know about people and places so far removed from her life. They simply could not understand why and how I was so knowledgeable or interested in politics and world affairs. They had, I suppose, never met the child of a consummate politician.

We breathed politics in our house; it consumed every aspect of our lives. Every election cycle was a period of excitement, hope, and expectation.

The politicians were the most confident of people; they were also— no matter that they were undoubtedly passionate about their causes and political beliefs—driven by a degree of ego; an exuberance of confidence that their party would be victorious. Later on, I learnt that this was an essential ingredient in the makeup and DNA of a successful politician. Why else would one put oneself through such a brutal exercise in what is,in simple terms, a competition to determine your popularity in the publicdomain and amongst the length and breadth of a nation? The popularity of your policies, your team, your own character and personality?

It was impossible not to be infected by the exhilaration and anticipation in the build-up to every election, in my house, from both my father and mother.

My mother was more than simply a politician's wife; she was as engrossed in politics as she was disgusted with the inevitable intrigues, petty jealousies, and bad blood, that seem to be an ingredient of politics and in politicians.

Were all of my siblings as fascinated by political events as Iwas? I am honestly not sure. I know I certainly was, gripped by all the anticipation.

My father, Chief S.O. Shonibare, as financial secretary of the Action Group, had been asked years earlier to develop an investment company for the party, along the lines of his own company, Shonny Investments and Properties Company, which by this time had evolved into a solid diverse business empire with interests in property, shipping (Nigerian Shipping Line), timber (Africa Timber Merchants), and trading (West African Associates). With partners from Iceland, they also imported stockfish, a luxury delicacy in many homes in Southern Nigeria.

Mobile Films, an ingenious advertising company concept, was as implied by its name, a mobile cinema. It would travel the length and breadth of rural Nigeria showing films, mostly Indian, to the excited villagers who would swarm to the grounds where the films were to be shown. The anticipation of watching these Indian films, that unique genre of love, dance, and magic, certainly gave them more excitement than anything they had ever imagined in their mundane rural life. In between the films, adverts of products that were being sold, or about to be sold in the villages were slotted in. As such, Mobile Films was also agenius way to launch and market political campaigns.

There was undoubted synergy in this myriad of companies. Playing a solid role in all of these investments was Lord Thomson of Fleet Street, the Canadian-born, British newspaper tycoon, who had a joint venture (JV) with the Action Group (AG) in the Amalgamated Press. Lord Thomson had once said of my father, "Shonibare had one of the most brilliant minds I have ever known."

The 1960 election was a pivotal moment in the lives of all Nigerians.As a key founding member of the Action Group and the party's financial secretary, my father's role was to arrange the financial resources to fund the ambitious political campaigns of the party that would culminate in the election that led to Nigeria's independence from the British in 1960.

I remember the innovative method of advertising the party and its candidate using helicopters with the words 'Action Group' and 'Awo' emblazoned in the skies. The excitement was palpable; there was absolutely no way, it had seemed, that the Action Group (AG) juggernaut would not sweep the whole country and bring our charismatic, visionary, policy wonk of a leader, Awolowo, to the helms of power…or so we thought!

I remember being so overwhelmed with excitement, so overwhelmed with the exhilaration of it all, that for many nights, I simply could not sleep.

The campaign over, all of Nigeria went to cast their votes to end British rule and usher in an independent Nigeria ruled by Nigerians—a disparate group, made up of two hundred and fifty ethnic groups speaking over five hundred languages.

The country had been clubbed together by the British Government,and christened in January 1897 by the British journalist, Flora Shaw, who later married Lord Lugard, the governor of Northern Nigeria Protectorate and the colony and protectorate of Southern Nigeria. He'd signed a document consolidating the two for the most ignominious of reasons: balancing the books of the two entities, or so it is widely believed, thereby creating the

Colony of Nigeria.

So naive of us all not to have anticipated the inevitable: that a nation bunched together in this manner and for this reason would struggle so painfully hard to become a viable nation-state; so terribly naive indeed. The culmination of its fight for independence was the election of 1960,a watershed moment in the history of Nigeria since its amalgamation bythe British in 1914.

I could barely contain myself; it was impossible not to get caughtup in the fever-pitch exhilaration that pervaded our home as we awaitedthe results of the election. It was the only conversation at our dinner table. Then came the unbearable anticipation of counting the votes, and thereafter, the results.

We were all glued to the radio as if our lives depended on it, listening in anxious trepidation as the results slowly poured in.

The Action Group swept the Western Region, the first set of results to be announced on the radio. A long, excruciating night lay ahead of us,and I remember going to bed exhausted, but elated, as my parents waitedto hear the results from the rest of the vast hinterland of our country.

I woke up the next morning to a house with a palpable sense of gloom and doom and bitter disappointment.

We had not won! It was a clean sweep by the NPC in the Northern states. Each announcement of the abysmal performance of the Action Group in these states was followed by '*ba ko daya*', which means 'zero' in Hausa. It was repeated again and again until the final gut punch—the party had lost its deposit to boot. The Action Group did make some headway in the Midwest and the Middle Belt whilst the NCNC had been victorious in most of the Eastern states.

NPC was the clear winner, the Action Group was first runner-up, and NCNC—which had now evolved as the preferred party for the eastern bloc, with its own charismatic leader, Dr Nnamdi Azikiwe—wasthird. All the cards were clearly stacked in favour of NPC and its leader,Sir Ahmadu Bello, the Sardauna of Sokoto, the clear favourite of the British, our colonial masters.

The results were followed by intense politicking between the three parties which, at that time, went way above my head. It culminated with the emergence of Sir Tafawa Abubakar Balewa as the first prime minister of Nigeria. I never could figure out how it was that the less rigid but equally charismatic leader of the NCNC, Dr Nnamdi Azikiwe,was able to forge an alliance with the Northern Party which secured his largely ceremonial position as President of Nigeria.

The system of government established post-independence wasa parliamentary one, following the tradition of the British. The Action Group, winning the second largest number of seats, became the official opposition party.

It was followed by a bitter internecine war within the Action Group, which culminated in strife, conflict, and hatred, ultimately becoming a major factor leading to the coup d'état in January 1966, andto the subsequent bitter Civil War in Nigeria from 1966 to 1970. A verydark period in the history of Nigeria. It is also the reason why, despite my passion for world politics and international relations, I, like every child of my mother, were warned from our early years to "never ever go into politics."

We all heeded her entreaties.

My half-brother, Supo Shonibare, who I am particularly close to, embraced politics heart and soul, throwing himself into it. He heeded the call, retaining our father's legacy in the Action Group. I am so terribly proud of him.

MOVE TO ENGLAND

Not long after this, we moved away from the house we'd called home, to the serene and ever so quiet Maryland Estate. My father had, by now, completed this residential estate he'd started building in 1955.

Over the years, he had completed the lovely estate, the first of its kind in Nigeria. My mother had added her indelible mark by planting coconut trees in boulevard fashion throughout the estate. Then they commenced work on their dream home, the Grecian-inspired Maryland Villa.

The move was such a dramatic one, but oddly enough, I do not have too vivid a memory of it other than too many things happening, being rather shell-shocked at the vastness of our new abode, but also its isolation, and no more neighbours popping in and out of our house on Spencer Street. My childhood friends no longer lived across the road, but I do remember we were all given new bikes, taught how to ride them, and had tremendous fun racing across the estate, and sometimes, into Ikeja GRA.

It was also not too long after our move to Maryland Estate that my parents made the decision, undoubtedly shaken by my nasty experience at

Reagan Memorial Baptist Primary School and the unfolding political unease in Nigeria, to send us all to school in England, bringing a definite end to one chapter of our lives.

Bearing in mind that during this era, circa 1960, just after Nigeria obtained its independence from Britain, Nigeria had many excellent schools steeped in the very best tradition of British education, why on earth had my father decided we must move to the UK and be educated as proper English young ladies?

As I grew older, I began to work out why my father—who was always so intuitive, so very many years ahead of his years, and is, alongwith Chief Obafemi Awolowo, one of the founding fathers of the ActionGroup—saw the writing on the wall. He foresaw that the bickering and power struggle between the leaders of the Action Group that broke out almost immediately after Nigeria obtained its independence in 1960 would ultimately become a full-blown war.

He had the wherewithal to get his children away from the toxicitythat soon consumed the whole political class. The five eldest girls were sent first, in 1961. I was ten years old at the time.

In mid-May 1961, we boarded the MV Aureol, one of the cruise liners of the British-owned Elder Dempster Shipping Line, and embarkedon our journey to the United Kingdom, to a totally new life. I was besidemyself with anticipation.

I was excited to travel with my whole family: my parents, all eight children, and my cousin, Sisi Bola. My father had adopted her and her sister, Bisi, when their father, my father's younger brother, was killed in a tragic car accident. They became part and parcel of my family.

Leading up to our date of departure, there seemed to be anunending packing of essential items we would need in England, particularly of food like yam, garri, and *elubo*.

Mr and Mrs Gleave were very close friends of my parents. Mr Gleave was a genius property surveyor. He acted as a consultant for all my parents' property transactions, and later, to the various property portfolio and developments of The Odu'a Investment Company, a conglomerate with substantial investments in real estate, printing and publishing, equipment leasing, food and beverages, agriculture and agribusiness, construction and manufacturing, hospitality, financial services, and oil and gas. It was conceived to be the holding company for the myriad of investments anddevelopments of the Action Group.

Mrs Gleave, Diane, was a gorgeous, elegant lady; she looked like a model, like she'd stepped straight out of a photoshoot from *Vogue*. They lived in the penthouse of the newly completed twenty-one-storey, ultra-modern high-rise, Western House, one of the first of its kind in Nigeria.

I remember the first time I visited their penthouse apartment in Western House. I was totally bowled over. Straight out of a feature in the luxury living section of *House and Garden*, with a spectacular view of the marina. A mixture of Manhattan, Park Lane, and a hint of Paris.

Diane Gleave asked my parents if she could take the girls shopping to get them ready for our sojourn to the UK, and they said, "yes." She took us to this awesome boutique on Lagos Island.

We were kitted out in purple velvet tulle dresses, with shoes to match. They were gorgeous. We did indeed feel and look like fairies.

Yes, we were ready for London and the brave new world that beckoned.

Yes, indeed, we were ready and roaring to go.

The day arrived. Loaded with our humongous baggage and crated foodstuff, we set off for Apapa Wharf where the cruise ship was moored. An army of family and friends were on hand to see us off.

It took ages to settle us all in our royal suite, and all the adjacent rooms needed to accommodate our large entourage of a family. Finally,the ship sounded its huge bugle to signal we were about to sail. Then, wewere off!

Our journey to Liverpool would take about two weeks, stopping at different ports across the West African coast: Monrovia in Liberia, Banjul in the Gambia, Las Palmas, and then, on to Liverpool. Our first port of call was Takoradi in Ghana.

There was an array of activities to do on the ship to amuse both us children of varying ages and our parents—tombola nightly, daily shows, dinner at the Captain's table, swimming, tennis, and more.

But there was a major problem. I was not used to the European diet. I craved *eba* or *amala* with okra or *ewedu* and stew. My ever-resourcefuland ingenious mother somehow managed to get me some *eba* and *ewedu*,

I'm still not quite sure how. Whilst this helped somewhat, and I was able to keep some food down, I was violently seasick throughout the journey. Even recalling the experience so many years later makes me nauseous.

No one could prepare us for the violent turbulence of the British Channel, only made bearable by the fact that everyone else was as sick and nauseated as I, and the assurance that we would soon be arriving in Liverpool.

At long last, we arrived at our destination. But what a profound disappointment it turned out to be. I was not impressed. The ghastly old buildings matched the dreary, damp weather.

We were again met by an array of family and friends who had come all the way from London to meet us.

From Liverpool, we took a train to London; the ride was a bit of ablur as I was exhausted from the long trip, but as we pulled up to EustonStation and were driven across London to our new home, my energy and excitement quickly returned.

London was certainly the gorgeous heaven I had spent endless nights anticipating and dreaming of as I waited with scarcely a bated breath most nights in my bed in Maryland Villa.

My parents had purchased a huge apartment located at 21 Kensington Court Gardens. It was beautifully decorated, and I wonderedif the elegant Mrs Greave had had something to do with it.

We wandered around our new home, thrilled to bits as we fought over who would sleep where. At last, we had arrived at our new home and were eager to embrace our new life.

By and large, I have to admit I was a pretty obedient child and did notbreak too many rules as a teenager.

My parents set some ground rules pretty early on:

Never ever must we hear you say, "Daddy, Mummy, don't be silly!" or disrespect your parents in any way, as British children are wont to do.

Do not eat sweets excessively and damage your teeth to the extentthat you end up with false teeth by the time you are thirty.

And repeatedly from Mummy:

A University education is an absolute must and non-negotiable; it is expected that every child achieves at least a first degree.

But I must admit, I hated boarding school in England.

It did not matter that the first schools had been carefully selected for us, by no less than Miss Gibson, Lord Thomson's super-efficient and meticulous secretary. I experienced overt racism for the first time in my life, from the teachers, even though we were treated like little maharajas by the very business-savvy principal of the small school in Surrey, Miss Auer. She was clearly blown over that on our admission, all five of us, my father had requested for the cost of our school fees plus other extras, and paid the lot, five years in advance!

Somehow, it was firmly etched in her mind that we were to be brought up as proper English ladies. We did all the extracurricularactivities she felt were essential to making young, anglicised ladies of us: horse riding, ballroom dancing, elocution, piano, and singing lessons. She, however, failed woefully in ensuring that she provided us her most important responsibility: her duty of care.

I'm still shaken by the memory of being picked on by this cruel, racist teacher who had selected me to take part in the Christmas Carol Service. I was to recite the poem *The Little Black Boy* by William Blake.

How does one erase from one's memory the abysmal humiliationof standing up to an audience of parents and students, giving a little curtsy, and saying the lines…

My mother bore me in the southern wild,
And I am black, but O! My soul is white;
White as an angel is the English child:
But I am black as if bereav'd of light.

I still remember the tears rolling down my face as I recited this poem, then rushing off the stage in a full flood of tears. It was undoubtedly the most humiliating experience of my life.

This encounter with blatant racism is one reason I relate so strongly with African Americans who continue to protest against institutional racism. The fact is racism runs rampant in the underbelly of most countries in Europe. In America, it is of pandemic proportions, and I believe it is long overdue for America, the so-called leader of the free world, to have an honest discussion about its long history of racism.

During our teenage years, I must admit we did break some rules, nothingout of the ordinary for a typical teenager. We regularly snuck out to the Cue (later 'Q') Club on Praed Street for ladies' night. The Cue Club wasone of the first black-owned clubs in the UK, playing a mix of soul, funk,ska, and reggae. It was really harmless fun; we learnt the latest dance moves and showed off our skills, relishing the attention we found from young Nigerian boys who were club regulars.

There were the 60s funk parties held on regular occasions at the iconic 1 South Villas, near the Camden Town area of London. It is difficult to articulate the extraordinary atmosphere at these parties which all the Young Turks, those who understood the rules, simply had to attend.

Come to think of it, I never did see South Villas during the day, onlyat night, with its dark red lights and psychedelic neon lights illuminatingthe house just enough to enable us see each other, and giving the South Villas a much grander look than what it probably was in the light of day.

Not everyone understood that you didn't have to wear the most expensive clothes or pose to be accepted at and enjoy those parties. The 60s were indeed a unique era; it was all about freedom, love not war, dance, and more love. Can the complicated world we live in now ever replicate the distinct vibe of the sixties? If only!

My outfits were simple enough. I wore black exclusively for mostof my teenage years, long before the goth look became fashionable. I just thought it was cool. In a way, it speaks to my propensity for creativity and originality. I am not easily influenced by trends.

I had a standard answer for everyone who asked me why I was forever dressed in black.

"Oh," I would respond. "I am mourning."

"Mourning what?"

"The lost cause." Don't ask me why. I just thought it was super cool.

A HOLIDAY OF A LIFETIME

Lord Thomson's secretary, Miss Gibson, was a rather stout woman who exuded kindness always and was my first introduction to an executive with exceptional organisational skills. She simply took care of everything that needed to be taken care of for her boss.

She organised an unforgettable summer holiday for us children inthe summer of 1964, six months after we had lost our father. My motherand Lord Thomson felt we, the children, needed to take our minds off our father's death, and that some pampering and distraction would help ease the pain.

And so, a holiday was planned for all six of us: the teenage girls aged eighteen, sixteen, and the twins, fourteen; our younger sister, twelve, and our little brother who was ten at the time.

Thinking about it even now, so many years later, it was indeed like a Hollywood-scripted holiday, three whole months of adventure, experiencing new, exciting places in Europe.

Our chaperone was our eldest sister, Ronke, who, though only eighteen years old, was the most conservative eighteen-year-old I have ever known. She missed out completely on the free-spirited sixties. She was a strict enforcer of all the rules our parents had set for us, but was also kind and caring. We all loved her to bits.

Don't eat too many sweets!

No talking to boys!

Don't forget whose children you are!

Somehow, she always got us in line, and we adhered to her rigid rules. Well, that is, most of the time.

Miss Gibson arranged our travel through Thomson Travels, ownedby Lord Thomson. The journey had a bit of a rocky start. We set off on a ferry crossing the channel. A more horrendous experience I cannot recall; I was violently seasick throughout. We arrived in Calais and were met by a Thomson Tours representative who arranged our next transfer. A representative of the agency was always there to meet us at every stopof our three-month adventure.

Our first port of call was Dinard in Brittany. Its beaches and lovely climate made it a popular tourist destination. We stayed, as we did on all the stops, in a five-star hotel. Like the true professional tour operators they were, Thomson Tours operators made sure to fill our days with fun-packed tours to unforgettable historic locations including St Malo and Mont St-Michel in Normandy, France. They also arranged some sportiveactivities, organising tennis lessons with professional tennis coaches.

We left Dinard and headed for Paris on the preferred mode of travel from destination to destination: high-speed luxury trains. I discovered, at last, one form of travel in which I did not suffer my usual violent motion sickness: travel by train! I loved it.

We took the night train, slept in very comfortable sleeping coaches, and arrived in Paris. This was one stop which, for some reason, I can barely recall, save for the lovely meals. Croissants and other delicious pastries at breakfast, and the delectable feasts with amazing sauces for lunch and dinner. I had got over being nauseated by European food.

Boarding the trans-European train from Paris, we travelled south, transferring in Nice, and were met, as always, by an ever-efficient representative from Thomson Holidays, ensuring a seamless transfer from departures to arrivals. Eventually, we arrived in Milan.

I can never forget my first impression of Milan. Enormous buildings, all dark and ugly, but the people looked so beautiful and incredibly elegant.

I have always been fascinated by the subtle changes in features that differentiated one ethnic group from another. I cannot recall how often my mother would say to me, "Stop staring, Taiwo!" as I gazed, completely captivated by the features of a newly discovered ethnic group.

I was spellbound by the faint but distinct changes in the look and features of the various people we came across during our European adventure. It never occurred to me then that we, a group of African teenagers in the summer of 1964, travelling first-class across Europe, must have been a topic of curiosity everywhere we went.

A HOLIDAY OF A LIFETIME

We arrived in Milan on a balmy evening. For some reason, my enduring recollection of the city forever etched in my memory, was the face of one ravishingly beautiful lady with stunning dark green eyes, dressed elegantly in a multi-coloured summer dress. Could she have been Sophia Loren?

From Milan, we separated as planned. My sister, who was two years older, my younger sister, two years younger, and I, proceeded to Rimini on the Adriatic coast in the Italian Riviera.

The other three—our big sister, my twin sister, and my younger brother—headed to Viareggio in Tuscany instead.

It was in Rimini that my teenage self had a taste of what it felt like to be chased around by young, hot-blooded Italian boys screeching,"*Bella. Bella.*" I was not the least bit flattered. Their persistence, frankly,terrified me.

In the end, I decided it was safer to keep to the beach during the day, and the confines of our hotel from there on, to avoid the unwanted attention of those uncouth boys.

From Rimini, our next destination was Innsbruck, Austria. We traversed the beautiful European landscape from Italy, marvelling at the spectacular Alps. We arrived at our destination, and I marvelled again at the change in the distinct ethnic look of the Bavarian people of Innsbruck in Austria.

The people we encountered were very friendly and naively innocent; we met some teenage boys who asked us in their faltering, broken English, "if you wash, will it not come off?" referring to thecolour of our skins. They had never in their lives seen a black person.

Honestly, we were not the least bit offended; they were earnest and genuinely curious.

Ever ingrained in my memory is the fact that the Austrians were the most well-mannered, cultured Europeans we met. Young ladiescurtsied to their elders and young boys bowed!

From the mountains of Innsbruck, we took the train to Vienna, and again enjoyed a stay at a five-star hotel. We took in all the tourist attractions; naturally, it included a visit to one of the famous Viennese classical music concerts, an unforgettable experience.

Our next and final stop was Amsterdam, Netherlands; definitely not one of my favourite stops in our long summer adventure in Europe. We arrived in chilly weather, and we had not packed warm clothes whenwe set off on our long summer adventure.

From Amsterdam, we made our way to Rotterdam where we tookthe ferry back to the UK, and I was reminded of my system's violent reaction to movement on water; as sick as a dog all the way. Despite that, nothing could take away from the amazing sense of pleasure. We relished that we had been so terribly privileged to experience a once-in-a-lifetimeadventure.

On our return, we got a rude shock from my mum who was waitingfor us in our home in London.

"My Lord!" she shrieked. "You have all gotten so fat."

With her in London were our close family friends, Tokunbo and Sister Ayo Awolowo.

Our mother took us aside and explained that they had also recently experienced trauma, the loss of their elder brother, Segun, in a tragic car accident, as well as the imprisonment of their beloved father, Chief Obafemi Awolowo, the leader of the Action Group, the opposition party in the fledgling new Nigerian democracy, a casualty in the fallout of the nascent power struggle within the Action Group.

She explained that they would be joining us at school in England and that they were family. From that day, Tokunbo, later Dr Tokunbo Awolowo, and Sister Ayo, became my sisters for life.

Following the death of our father, my ever so wise mum decided we needed to appreciate that life had changed fundamentally.

We still lived in our expansive, five-bedroom apartment in a highbrow neighbourhood in Kensington, London, where our neighbours included the celebrated author, playwright, and poet, T.S. Eliot. Although he lived in our neighbourhood at the same time we were there, we never met him.

She decided to separate all of us from St Mary's Hill, a small public school in Horsell, Woking in Surrey, where we had been educated our first three years in England. Truth be told, we had all been rather indulged by the principal, Miss Auer, who seemed more intent on developing proper English ladies than ensuring we received the best possible education. It seems utterly ridiculous, come to think about it now, that we had to curtsy anytime we passed by her in the corridor.

The school devoted an overwhelming amount of energy and time to pupils learning ballroom dancing, elocution, and horse riding, all verywell, but my wise mother decided we needed a total paradigm shift, which was why she changed our schools, placing us in different schools.Her main objective for us was one thing and one thing only: passing ourexams and enrolling in a good university.

I had a miserable time in the new schools, experiencing intense racism, worse than I had ever been exposed to since arriving in England some four years earlier. I changed schools frequently, as my darling mother—as strict as she was—just couldn't bear to see her children so unhappy.

She removed me from one particular school, Penrhos College in Colwyn Bay, North Wales, because she had not considered just how far away it was from home. I hadn't complained to her, accepting that all boarding schools were like prisons. I'd long since resigned myself to the fact that I owed it to my mother to suffer and smile, to just bear it as best as I could and get on with it.

But within two days of visiting me, my mother—who was stayingin a hotel in Llandudno, a coastal town in North Wales—felt depressed and lonely. She couldn't shake off a deep melancholy, and coincidentally,kept hearing over and over on the radio, the famous number-one hit songat the time, *I Want to Go Home* by the Beach Boys.

"How can you bear this, my husband?" she asked me. She decidedher daughter was not returning to such a depressing place. I switched schools for the third time since I left St Mary's Hill, attending Headington School in Oxford, where she'd had a measure of success with one of my siblings. Kehinde and I both enrolled in the school for our A levels. She studied Science while I studied Humanities—History, English, and Government.

HOMECOMING

Having spent the better part of our childhood and teenage years in England, my mother decided we absolutely had to come back to Nigeria to attend university. In early September 1969, we arrived at Lagos International Airport (later renamed Murtala Mohammed International Airport). It was quite a shock to see the state of the place.

The 'airport' was really a shanty hall with long, wooden tables—the conveyor belts—where suitcases rolled on and off, and from where one would collect one's luggage.

I certainly stood out like a sore thumb in my 'micro-mini' and knee-length white socks, the quintessential Biba (the popular boutiqueat the time, on High Street, Kensington, London) outfit of the sixties teenager. We could feel people staring at us, shocked at our mini dresses,and not caring if we knew it too.

I wasn't as fluent in Yoruba as I'd been many years earlier, beforeour move to the UK, but the shock and dismay at our outfits was quite blatant.

I knew then that I was entering a world that would be starkly different from the one I had lived in for the last eight years, but I wastotally determined to embrace it.

I attended the University of Lagos—a premier university in Nigeria and one of the most competitive in the country to be admitted into—majoring in French, History and Political Science. The campus had beautiful edifices I was quite taken by. I later learnt the campus was modelled after some university in Eastern Europe which, I suppose, explains the uniquedesign of the older structures.

Throughout my years as a student, I never lived on the campus. How I envied all the new students who had naturally formed cliques; many had been classmates while attending schools like Queens College, St Anne, Holy Child College, and International School, Ibadan, some ofthe top secondary schools in the country at the time. I had some regret that I'd missed out on the unique experience of high school in Nigeria.

Nevertheless, I was determined to integrate myself and make new friends, no matter what it took. I made a conscious effort to walkup to everyone I came across and introduce myself. In this manner, I made my first friend, Eniola Bode Thomas, at the university. She was a freshman studying Law and we got along swimmingly. She was popularand seemed to know everyone, and I made sure to tag along with her, asmuch as possible, to social events.

"Hi! I am Taiwo," was my trademark introduction. It was easyto disarm people with my friendliness. This was not what they had anticipated from me, because I stood out, with my unique style, and I suppose, arriving at school every morning in a car, as most students lived on campus.

Some students would make fun of me. They would shout, "Football season has started again!" a reference, I assume, to my knee-length socks, which I wore with my mini dresses to hide the sores that covered my legs, the result of relentless mosquito bites. Mosquitoes just seemed to relish my fresh skin.

I had to contend with the natural animosity towards someonewho looked and sounded different, which I was, sadly, accustomed to from my time as a student in England. I was mortified that I was being subjected to a similar kind of snobbery in my own country, albeit more of an inverted snobbery. They were determined to snub me, and I was equally determined to make friends with them all.

I admit that sometimes, I felt alone, and now and then, I resented having been sent to school in England, completely missing out on the natural camaraderie the various cliques of students seemed to share.

During my first year in university, I helped establish, and was elected the president of, the French society. As president, I was invited to be an interpreter during state visits to Nigeria by Francophone leaders.

Through this network, I had the opportunity to visit BeninRepublic and Togo; quaint francophone countries neighbouring Nigeria.

I always looked forward to those trips; there was a certain *je ne saisquoi* about visiting those places, a feeling of being transported to a little rural village in France. You were guaranteed a great meal and authenticFrench patisserie.

It was during one of such visits to Cotonou, the capital of Dahomey (now known as Benin Republic), that I came across Diouf, a Cotonou- based Senegalese jeweller.

Ever my mother's daughter, I had a love of jewellery in my blood,but never matched her passion for them, I must admit. I seized on the opportunity to strike a deal with the Senegalese jeweller.

I decided to focus on gold rings made in the unique filigree craftsmanship of the Senegalese, and 'V' rings, very popular at the time though more common with Liberians.

I was nineteen years old when I started selling gold rings. At first,I thought my friends at university would be interested in buying, but as it turned out, most students could simply not afford them, although I thought the prices I offered were very reasonable. I enlisted Eniola BodeThomas to help sell the rings. She was able to sell some and make a quickbuck.

My real market was my mother's friends who not only patronisedme but were surprised by, and in awe of, my new entrepreneurial venture.They bought for themselves and their daughters, and I was able to quicklyturn my little jewellery business around, to the delight of my Senegalese jeweller, whilst enjoying the money I made from this opportunistic enterprise.

I was, to be honest, more chuffed than anything else.

So this is how you make money, I thought. *How easy! How fun!*

If only I was more prescient. If only I recognised that this was simply beginner's luck!

I ended up making lifelong friends at the University of Lagos. I also met the love of my life, Ladi. We had a few ups and downs, as in any long-term relationship, but we got married a couple of years after we'd both graduated. I acquired my name, Taiwo Taiwo; my unique, special name which I carry like a badge of honour till today.

THE MARYLAND HOTEL AND THE BEACHCOMBER NIGHTCLUB

The 1st of April, 1974, was my first day of work at the Maryland Hotel. Fresh out of the Ecole Hôtelière de Genève, the prestigioushotel management school in Geneva, I took over the management of the hotel, which was a fully owned subsidiary of Shonny Investmentsand Properties. It had been established, following my father's death in 1964, as the Maryland Guest House.

My mother was in a quandary about what to do with the sprawling Maryland Villa—the Grecian-inspired home set on four acres of land on Maryland Estate—she had shared with my father. It was a resplendent property, but impractical for a young widow with eight young children, six of whom were in boarding schools in the UK.

After the death of my father, my mother assumed complete controlof the business, keeping his dreams alive.

First, she had to figure out what to do with the guest houses, eightself-contained bedroom suites, each with a living room, as well as the detached two-bedroom guest house, all independent of the main villa. Her long-time confidante and family lawyer, Mr Akin Lawrence, gave her the brilliant idea of converting the guest houses into a proper lodging for paying guests, with a restaurant and bar. The Maryland Estate was situated on Airport Road near the international airport, positioning the guest houses to serve the burgeoning airline business. The conversion proved to be a wise, viable one, and very profitable. Within a couple of years, she expanded the thirteen guest houses into the fifty-room Maryland Hotel.

Our foray into the nightclub business began on a hilarious note. After completing the new sixty-room Maryland Hotel, a complex comprising fifty double rooms, and ten new single rooms, she invited Mr Vendish, a Nigerian-based German interior designer who came highly recommended, to conceptualise, design, build and furnish the bar and restaurant. He had free rein to do as he pleased with the space.

Designed by the architect, Arc Lai Balogun of Modular Group, the bar and restaurant area was quite expansive; rather inappropriately large for a hotel bar and restaurant. The size of the space coupled with its cone-shaped roof meant conceptualising the interior design was going to be a bit of a challenge.

My mother allowed him to get on with it uninterrupted—apart from groaning and gasping as the cost of the project shot up repeatedly. To Mr Vendish, she really must have been a made-in-heaven client, as she hardly ever checked in on him to see what he was doing.

A few months later, it was completed and Mr Vendish proudly presented to my mother…a fabulous, 70s-themed nightclub he named The Beachcomber! Attached to it was a standalone, exquisitely decorated La

Parisienne restaurant. That was the end of his work, and the beginningof a ton of work for us as, willy-nilly, he'd thrown us into the nightclub business, a business we knew very little about, and to boot, forced us intoa high-end restaurant business we were equally unqualified to manage.

The decision had already been made that I would run the Maryland Hotel after I graduate from the University of Lagos in 1973. Earning a Bachelor's degree in French and History, I had dreams of joining the Foreign Service. It aligned with my love for meeting and engaging with new people, especially people from different countries and cultures, but I strongly felt it was my duty to support my mother at the time. I researched the best colleges where I could learn more about the hotel industry. In the end, after serving a year in the compulsory National Youth Service Corps, I applied and was admitted into Ecole Hôtelière de Genève in Geneva, Switzerland.

I never discussed salary, emoluments, terms of a contract, or job description, when I started working at the hotel. Every single salary advance, review, and contract of service, was always at the insistence of my mother.

I was determined to make a great impression, especially on our long-serving managers: the ever-reliable and loyal Mrs Animashaun, a Jamaican married to a Nigerian; and the hardworking General Manager of the company, Mr Morakinyo Bajomo, who had started his career at UAC, and had been brought in by my father to be his Executive Secretaryand right-hand man when he created Shonibare Estate and formedShonny Investments and Properties.

Driven by the need to not be dismissed as an indulged daughter of their boss who had been brought in simply because of who her parents were, I was at my desk at 7.30 every morning, raring to go.

I was extremely humble, listening attentively as they took me through the processes of the business and around every room in the Maryland Hotel. I got a tour of the nightclub, the restaurant, and finally,a tour of the various properties on Maryland Estate.

It's strange that despite my close relationship with the management staff, especially Mrs Animashaun, we continued to address each other formally; perhaps it was a sign of the times. I was always Miss Shonibare, and later, Mrs Taiwo, and she ever remained Mrs Animashaun. She taught me the ropes of bookkeeping and the essential skill of balancing our books, which was, yes, important work, but pure drudgery!

I was eager to make an impact with the knowledge I had gained from my unique experiences at the Ecole Hôtelière de Genève. I embarked on an intensive training programme, beginning with the catering department of La Parisienne.

They were taught how to lay a table fit for a king. *Service à l'anglaise? Service à la française?* They learnt it all, taking pride in the culinary knowledge they were gaining. We held weekly tests for the catering staffto assess their ability to grasp new concepts and methods that would ensure the restaurant met the world-class standards we set for it.

I taught them everything they needed to know about wines, including which wine was most suitable for meats, birds, and fish. Theyknew the difference between a Bourgogne, a Bordeaux, and a Claret, andwere even knowledgeable about various French vineyards.

I would order an impressive range of fine French wines from Brian Munro, the efficient wholesaler who supplied us an array of goods, groceries, and toiletries, but also had an extensive wine list. It's amazing what was available on the market: Gevrey-Chambertin, Nuits-Saint-Georges, and more superb wine selections.

Was all this effort really necessary? I do know that when the hotel industry exploded with the construction of the Holiday Inn on Victoria Island (which later became Eko Le Meridien, and is now known as Eko Hotels), the people I had trained were, one by one, head hunted, and became the pioneering staff at some of these hotels. Vincent, one of the smartest of my trainees, who later became my personal assistant, eventually relocated to New York, staying and excelling in the hotel industry over there. He is now a top manager with the Marriott Group, and has kept in touch, visiting me on his occasional trips to Nigeria.

He keeps me regaled by his anecdotes on the life-changing experiences, lessons and knowledge, he'd acquired under my tutelage at the Maryland Hotel. I was bemused when he said that every time he passes a wine shop in New York, and he spots a bottle of Bordeaux, he thinks of me!

It had been instilled in me that I was expected to play multiple roles; as my mother used to say, "Anywhere that needs to be cleaned, we all get our brooms out and start sweeping." In other words, if there was any area of our business that had an issue, it was my job to go in, roll up my sleeves, and fix the problem.

The General Manager running the very successful Beachcomber nightclub, left us in the lurch without notice, deciding to explore other opportunities and take his talent elsewhere. I had no choice but to get out the 'broom' and find a solution, which meant adding 'running the Beachcomber' to my job description.

After finishing my day job running the hotel, restaurant, and whatever needed done, I would head home, change my outfit, and leavefor the club.

At that point, I was happily married. A couple of months after joining Shonny Investments and Properties Co., on 6 September 1974,I married my college sweetheart and had my first child, a son, Ladipo, ayear later.

Ever determined to set a good example, and above all, not wanting anyone to say I did not merit the position I was given, I worked up to the very day I went into labour, and was back at work six weeks later. I'd even scheduled, a week after giving birth to my son, business meetings in neighbouring Benin Republic and Cote d'Ivoire in search of a new executive chef for La Parisienne, as the Swiss chef had proven to be a disaster.

I did not enjoy running the Beachcomber. Ladi wasn't too thrilled either, putting his foot down about going with me to the nightclub; the idea of staying up all night, after a full day at his law practice, understandably, did not appeal to him.

But what could we do? We needed someone to take chargefollowing the unexpected exit of the General Manager. I did what had to be done for the club, and successfully too, for a while. Thankfully, mymother—God bless her—stepped in, approaching my younger brother, Alaba, who had been with the company for some time, and was primarilyresponsible for managing our residential estates.

She said, "Listen. Taiwo is married. She graciously accepted this additional duty, but I think it is only right that you take over."

His reaction was typical, making certain demands before he accepted the job. First, he insisted that his weekends were sacrosanct. Healso asked to be paid fifty percent of the takings at the gate. My mother reminded him I'd been doing the job for a year, never asking for a pennyto be added to my salary at the Maryland Hotel.

"Well," he'd responded. "That's Taiwo, not me. She doesn't need money; I do. Besides, she is a woman."

His demands were met and he took over the weekend running of the Beachcomber, collecting fifty percent of the takings at the gate. The Beachcomber operated as a nightclub only during the weekends. During the weekdays it was a bar, a very plush one frequented by guests staying in the hotel, and residents of Maryland Estate and its environs.

I moved through every department of the hotel; to this day, I'm grateful for the invaluable and unparalleled lifelong business knowledge I acquired from my experiences working there.

Running the Maryland Hotel and its various departments wasthe best hands-on training I could ever receive. Hotel management is very demanding, entailing round-the-clock production of meals, barand room service, twenty-four-hours-a-day maintenance to ensure the smooth running of the hotel.

Incredible as it might seem, until as recently as 1977, there were only seven hotels and guest houses in the city of Lagos—Maryland Hotel, Airport Hotel, the rather dubious Niger Palace Hotel in Yaba,

Mainland Hotel, Bristol Hotel, and the most popular, Federal Palace Hotel, established in readiness for Nigeria's independence in 1960.

With competition growing quickly, I decided we needed to re- launch Maryland Hotel. I conceptualised giving the hotel a makeover, cosmetically enhancing the rooms, and adding a brand-new standout reception area.

My mother was away overseas when I undertook this ambitious project, which was done on a minimal budget. When she returned, she was awestruck by all the changes we'd made.

"Taiwo, my husband! You are something else," she said as she inspected the renovated rooms. It's amazing how much her encouragement spurred me on to do more.

The loss of her husband when she was forty-one years old, leaving hera widow with eight children to look after, was undoubtedly a defining moment in my mother's life.

It took her will of steel, an unflappable ability to analyse issues and forge the right solutions that, in the end, helped her deal with the seemingly insurmountable problems she encountered—mainly involving their various businesses—following my father's death.

She navigated financial crises, treachery even, and problems withher teenage children, all of whom were being educated in very expensive schools in the UK.

She would recount stories of receiving bills for school fees, not knowing how she was going to pay them all. She'd write to the schools to bargain for more time. One delay tactic she used, which surprisingly proved effective, was requesting the school bill, which she already had in her possession, to buy more time!

But through it all, she kept going, and by 1969, she'd finished paying back the huge loans which were used to finance the constructionof the Maryland Estate, totalling £250,000, to Barclays Bank DCO.

In 1970, she embarked on an ambitious venture; she acquired interest in Elephant House from the Pearse family. Located on Broad Street, the original Elephant House was widely recognised as a fascinating example of Brazilian architecture in Nigeria. One of the conditions attached to her acquiring the building was if any other building was erected there, it must be called 'Elephant House'. The building she acquired was the first Elephant House, a historical monument reputable people like the architect, John Godwin, fought very hard to have listed.

It took ten years to get permission to build our Elephant House because, in those days, the Lagos State Government had strict conditions in place for building high-rises. There had to be a fifty-feet setback in front, and fifty feet on the sides. A survey of the impact of the construction on the environment also had to be done, and what is now called an Environmental Impact Analysis had to be submitted. Due to the relatively modest size of the land surrounding the Elephant House building, to meet state requirements, my mother had to acquire three more plots to make up the 2,502.52 square metres of the present Elephant House. It took her ten years to get the approval, and she always contended that that was the hardest part of the process. Once she did, she handed it over to me to raise the needed funds for the project.

I was just twenty-nine years old, but it didn't matter to her. She reminded me that my father was very young when he put the Western House together, one of his many properties.

ELEPHANT HOUSE

The first Elephant House project meeting I attended was at the offices of Arc Lai Balogun of Modular Group. Arc was the young, mercurial architect who had succeeded the older architects, Nickson and Borys, who, frustrated with the approval process, eventually pulled out. Nickson and Borys, the original architects charged with designing the building, had found the process of obtaining approvals from the labyrinth of government agencies to construct an eighteen- storey modern high-rise on Broad Street—the centre of the prime business district of Lagos Island—daunting and exhausting.

Ever ready to prove I was not some silly girl who had been draftedinto their serious team of professionals to handle an enormous twenty- one-million-dollar project, I was focused. With a notebook and pen in hand, I absorbed everything, jotting down all the salient points.

I had learnt very early in my career that one of the greatest folliesis pretending to know or understand something you do not, so I was never shy about asking for explanations of jargon used by professionals in their discipline, words that were double dutch to me. I was always amused to find that many of the other participants in the meeting were usually as ignorant about the meaning of various terminology used as I was, whilst nodding their heads in feigned comprehension. On the contrary,I discovered that letting professionals know you do not understand the specialised language they used, and asking for clarity, always in the end,earned you some level of respect.

We worked with an array of professional consultants: the architects of Modular Group; the team of structural engineers at Adeyemi Ogundipe and Partners; the electrical engineering company, Tee Associates; mechanical engineering firm, Dezyntek, with its principal, Dr Olunloyo; and Group Q Associates, the team of quantity surveyors, withChief Odumosu as principal.

Arc Balogun of Modular Group was the head of the project and had been given the special dispensation of selecting all the consultants, who were all, indeed, true professionals. I was in awe of him at the commencement of the project. We never considered that he had personally selected all the consultants for the project without any input from us; nor did we think anything of the fact that they were his cronies.

However, as the project progressed, I became much less enamoured of him. It was difficult to forgive him for not attending a single site meeting once the project started. My mother especially, and to a lesser degree I, also felt this was very disrespectful.

A multi-million-dollar eighteen-storey high-rise, in the centre of Lagos, was an edifice any architect would be proud to be associated with, proud to play a part in designing and constructing. I could not understand why he would treat the project and us, his clients, in such a cavalier manner. But to be fair, and to his credit, he had, by and large, assembled an extremely professional team who were determined to execute the project to the very best of their abilities.

It seemed astonishing that ten years into the project, feasibility studies had never been carried out. It was during one of our meetings that a consultant advised that we needed to have a 'visibility' report prepared at once!

I suppose his terminology was apt; after all, the feasibility report would lead to the project becoming visible.

The unanimous decision was made to commission Alan Shelley, managing partner of Knight Frank & Rutley (KFR), to prepare the report. We were all confident he was the best person to deliver a bankable feasibility report for the project. That is how I came to know Alan, who became my mentor, teaching me everything I know about properties. He played a pivotal role in my successful supervision of the construction of Elephant House, a complex, modern, multi-million-dollar building, a feat I accomplished at just twenty-nine years old.

Alan had a fascinating background, as did his lovely wife, Joey. He'd come to Nigeria to join the British Overseas Office, a young man—about eighteen years old—straight out of school with nothing more than his school certificate. He was posted to serve at the Nigerian Railways.

He was allocated official living quarters in the Railway compound,an enormous, fully-furnished bungalow with a living room and multiple bedrooms. He'd been surprised by how much space and furniture he'd been given as it was just him staying there.

That was just the beginning. Shortly after he arrived, he was informed he was entitled to a car.

A car? he'd thought. *But I can't drive! Besides, how will I ever pay for it?* He was assured it wouldn't be a problem as he would also be given a carloan and a car allowance to pay off the loan. He was flabbergasted.

He would tell me that this was not long after World War II, a warthat had devastated the UK and left many families in poverty, which putsinto context just how surprising it was that he'd been offered so much. Typically, a young man of his age would be living with his parents in a house, often without an indoor bathroom, with an outside Water Closet serving as a toilet. Also, it was highly unlikely that even a graduate from Oxford or Cambridge at the time could afford a car or pay off a car loan.

Alan Shelley flourished in Nigeria, meeting and marrying his soulmate, Joey, while in the country. He became a chartered surveyor and formed a partnership with the renowned UK residential and commercial estate agency, Knight Frank & Rutley (KFR). Alan understood property better than anyone I have ever met.

He had such a formidable reputation in the property market that he could conclude the capital funding required for a major property transaction over lunch at the Metropolitan by inviting, say, John in United Bank for Africa (UBA), Sam in First Bank of Nigeria (FBN), and Françoise in International Bank for West Africa (IBWA), and convincing them with his sheer knowledge about the prospects of the project. All the stakeholders needed was Alan's reassurance that the transaction wassolid;

and although this may seem a hyperbolic statement to make, he was never wrong.

The meeting with Alan took place in the boardroom of the KFR office; my mother and I were in attendance, and possibly, her personal lawyer, Mr Lawrence, too. Alan had read our brief and had a good grasp of the project before we met. I soon discovered he was very meticulous, always doing his homework diligently before any meeting.

I was instantly struck by his eyebrows, the bushiest eyebrows I had ever seen! He was warm, not at all intimidating, but nevertheless, very business-like.

The first question he asked took me aback.

"Why on earth do you want to build an eighteen-storey office block?"

I was shocked, especially as unbeknownst to Alan, our architects had even been contemplating going further—manipulating our existing approval for an eighteen-storey office block into a twenty-one-storey office block.

After Nigeria's independence in 1960, Lagos had gone throughan eclectic boom and halt in the construction of modern office spaces. My father had played a pivotal role in conceptualising and executingthe first wave of modern high-rises in Nigeria in his role as Managing Director of the Nigerian Investment Promotion Commission (NIPC). Hedeveloped the Wemabod Estates; the twenty-one-storey Western Houseon Broad Street; the multi-storey Investment House on the Marina; the Development House in Apapa; the twenty-three-storey Cocoa House in Ibadan, and a host of other property investments.

Construction of new projects halted during the tumultuous post-independence years which were coloured by political chaos in the country and culminated in the military coup of 1966, which in turn, led to the three-year civil war. The war ended in January 1970 and was quickly followed by the oil boom.

Alan explained, "Listen. If you build a ten-storey office block,I can be reasonably certain that it will be completed within twelve to sixteen months. With that certainty, I can guarantee that I will get you tenants right away to lease every inch of the vacant office space as soonas you move to site.

They will pay you one year in advance for the whole building, releasing cash flow for construction. When you get to the top floor, in effect with the shell of the building completed, they will pay you the remaining two years in advance with which you can complete the building, and voila, with very little debt you would have acquired a multi-million-dollar asset. With enough to move on to your next project.

But," he added. "An eighteen-storey high-rise is a completely different proposition. It cannot be completed in less than three years minimum, and the property market is such that it's impossible for meto predict what factors might be in place in three years which could fundamentally change the projections!"

Genius! In one sentence Alan taught me the most profound lesson I could ever have learnt about property investment, he became my mentor for life. Never allow yourself to get carried away by your architect's exotic design. Always ask yourself the question, "How will this detail improve my rent?" Be extremely firm, and never waiver. If your architect desires to squander money on ridiculous details to indulge his fantasies, let himdo so on his own project and at his cost, not yours!

I was eager to learn everything I could from him. I read all my notes after every meeting, and made sure I had a good grasp of everything discussed, even the most technical of details. I'm sure I must have been a thorough bore to my husband and friends as I loved nothing more than to show off my new-found knowledge of the technical side of building a high-rise.

We, the entire team involved in the project, all had a shared goal of trying to build the best state-of-the-art building we could, in the most creative manner possible, and using the most innovative concepts.

After extensive discussions, analysis and brainstorming, we decided to enlist the services of Dr Meshida of Nigerian Soil Engineering Company, soil foundation specialists and contractors. A distinguished gentleman with a mop of grey hair, he was an erudite and brilliant engineer.

He convinced us to employ what, at that time, was very much cutting-edge technology—building up the foundation with 'vibro fluctuation compactions', and not the traditional system of piling. It hadthe added benefit of being a fraction of the cost of piling, and could be completed within a much shorter time frame.

Ever the eager student, I learnt as much as I could about the technique and ~~could~~ describe what was, in effect, a technical system of creating a foundation for a high-rise by compacting sand and shakingit to fill the levels, creating a solid base for a building the size of the eighteen-storey Elephant House.

With the foundation quickly completed, the next and critical stageof the process involved the herculean task of raising the funds needed to finance the project.

FUNDING THE CONSTRUCTION

Armed with our feasibility study from the guru himself, Alan Shelley, which envisaged us limiting our borrowing, and proposed a scenario where rent payments would be received one year in advance as we built upwards to the top floor, with two years rent coming in to complete the project.

In all fairness, Alan did warn that he could not guarantee scenarios would not change, bearing in mind the three-year timeline anticipated for the construction, but Knight Frank & Rutley (KFR) did sign a document to confirm the intended plan of action for completing the project. What a pretty worthless document that proved to be when we eventually reached the top floor and requested rent payments only to be told they had not a single tenant!

It never fails to amaze me that till this date, banks routinely ask for this pointless document, confirmation of off-takers as a condition precedent for granting building loans. Totally ridiculous.

FUNDING THE CONSTRUCTION

The next expert who came recommended was Otunba Subomi Balogun. He had recently established City Securities Limited (CSL) and was making waves in the capital market. He was extremely warm and friendly, and I quickly learnt we had some kind of familial relationship through my father.

I believe he was impressed that I was so eager to learn, that I was single-minded and committed to seeing the success of the project.

CSL prepared the information memorandum for the project, and we agreed on a strategy for raising the needed capital.

My mother and I had previously been in discussions with First Bank, the biggest commercial bank in Nigeria at the time. We'd met with their brilliant Managing Director, Mr Samuel Asabia, through the kind introduction of the Ooni of Ife, the urbane, affable, international businessman with vast interests in a myriad of businesses, who also happened to be the traditional ruler of the cradle of Yorubaland, Ile Ife.

We could really only advance our discussions after we had completed the feasibility study and prepared a bankable information memorandum. We had also contributed the mandatory cash equity required by the owner/financier of the project to the promoter, includingall the above, plus the cost of the foundation.

Raising the six million naira (₦6,000,000) bridge finance was relatively easy. Otunba Balogun and his team at CSL achieved this relatively quickly, within six months.

I attended every one of these meetings; indeed, I wouldn't have missed them for the world. At some point, my mother stopped accompanying me.

"I have done the hard job," she'd told me. "Your father raisedthe capital to build huge multimillion-dollar projects when he was barely older than you are now. I have spent a fortune giving you the besteducation in the world, so prove it!"

She knew me well; saying and repeating those things reminded meI simply could not fail. I attended all the meetings, understood the projectlike the back of my hand, and was completely versed in our financial plan and the strategies we had in place for raising the capital.

Raising the bridge finance (three-year loans) from commercial banks, and assembling the consortium of lenders through the expert and professional guidance of CSL, under their formidable chairman, Otunba Subomi Balogun, was fairly straightforward. First Bank of Nigeria (FBN), United Bank for Africa (UBA), and International Bank for West Africa (IBWA), now known as the defunct AfriBank, committed to investing in the bridge finance of the project within months.

Raising the long-term finance was much trickier. The debenture stock, which all the bridge financiers insisted we had in place to take them out at the end of the three-year term of their loan, was a condition precedent before drawdown. I was getting very familiar with all the banking jargon.

It looked impossible; we just couldn't secure the long-term finance required to pull the project together. But I had an idea. I asked Uncle Subomi Balogun if I could give it a shot myself, and he responded that I could and should do everything possible to solve the issue.

I turned to my secret back-up: young, smart investment bankers, all friends of my husband. Most had won the Afro-American scholarships available to the smartest students in the best secondary schools inNigeria. They had earned their undergraduate degrees from prestigious American colleges including MIT, Berkeley, and UCLA, and had proceeded to Ivy League graduate schools like Harvard and the Sloan School of Management, to study what at that time, was a relatively newdiscipline—Master's in Business Administration (MBA).

They were, in effect, the first crop of investment bankers in Nigeria, and it was my great fortune that they were our dear friends.

Many had worked as investment bankers in institutions suchas Chase, City Bank, and Citibank of Chicago. They had all recently relocated to Nigeria and were working in management positions in the fledgling investment banks popping up in the country. I owe a debt of gratitude to our dear friends, Ayo Olagundoye, Ebi Banigo, and Ade Coker.

Most of my conversations with friends and family inevitably revolved around the construction of the Elephant House, especially my frustration with raising the long-term capital. I actively sought out theseinvestment bankers to seek their opinions and advice on how they wouldapproach raising the darn long-term funds without which we were not going to get a penny of the bridge finance already raised primarily by our financial advisers on the project, City Securities Limited.

It is to their credit that my eyes were opened to another sourceof funding none of our advisers had mentioned, not once: insurance companies. I was informed that these companies have long-term funds in their portfolio and would be looking for safe and secure investments with seven-year yields to match their portfolio.

They went beyond that, God bless them. One friend went out of his way to speak with an investment manager in Crusader Insurance, telling him about our project and setting up a meeting.

I knew my project and finance plan exceptionally well; with all modesty, I would get an A+ if I sat an exam on it. I met with investment managers of various insurance companies, with meetings set up through these supportive friends. I would rattle on about every aspect of the Elephant House project, letting them know how long their money would be in for and when it would be required.

I got a yes at almost every presentation, but to be honest, I wonderedif they really understood what I was talking about. They seemed more fascinated with my in-depth knowledge of the project, and how well I articulated my plan and vision for Elephant House.

I have to admit I did affect an anglicised accent during my presentations. I suppose on some level, I knew intuitively that doing so could help my cause. I was ready to use every weapon I had, and it certainly seemed to have worked.

I went the length and breadth of Broad Street, scheduling multiple meetings to sell my project. My husband, Ladi, whose firm, Abdulai Taiwo & Co., was acquiring a formidable reputation in the capitalmarket, played an invaluable role in giving the final push to some of those institutions, and ensuring we got a 'yes.'

That is how we got NICON, Niger Insurance, Crusader, African Alliance, British American, Marine and General, Nigerian General,Unity Life, Amicable Insurance, Guinea Insurance, and United Nations Information Centres (UNIC), to invest in the Elephant House project debenture loan stock, in amounts ranging from ₦1,000,000 to ₦750,000 to ₦500,000 to ₦200,000, with a total of ₦5,500,000 (five million, five hundred thousand naira) signed on to the Elephant House debenture stock, on the condition that we immediately paid them a 1% commitment fee to guarantee their commitment to fund and take out accrued balancesof the capital of the bridge financiers on completion of the development,and to guarantee their commitment to fund in the amount stated on the take out of the banks who had provided bridge finance.

I had a humbling and humiliating lesson to learn before completingthis part of the project.

The Bank of Credit and Commerce (BCCI) through their investment manager, the ever-affable Sammie Ojikutu, had committed to taking up ₦1 million in the consortium of bridge financiers. First Bank of Nigeria had committed ₦2 million, United Bank for Africa, ₦2 million, and IBWA, ₦1 million.

I received a last-minute call from Sam asking me to come overto their offices in Apapa, his bosses needed to clarify some issues on theloan.

I arrived promptly, as usual, on the dot of 8 a.m.—probably morelike 10 minutes to 8—and sat, waiting patiently to be called in, watchingthe clock move like a scene from an Alfred Hitchcock movie.

9 o' clock, 10 o' clock, 11 o' clock, 12 o' clock, 1 o' clock... Sammie would pop in periodically to let me know I hadn't been forgotten.

2 o' clock, 3 o' clock, 4 o' clock, 5 o' clock... I was called in by the Managing Director, Mr Raza—a Pakistani—who informed me, without missing a beat, that Sammie should not have committed BCCI to our project, a property investment. *They simply do not do that!*

I was flabbergasted and on the verge of tears. That was two days before a scheduled completion board meeting of our bridge and long- term lenders.

I informed him that pulling out at this stage could well jeopardisethe whole project, giving some other lenders the jitters and a forebodingsense that there might be some issues with the project. But he didn't budge.

Sammie took me aside and whispered that he felt because I was so young, it might be his bosses simply couldn't believe someone my age was 'the owner' of such a huge project, and thought there might be something suspicious about the set-up.

He also, rather unethically, gave me his boss's home address in Victoria Island.

"Go meet him with your mother tonight," he said.

I raced to Ikeja, told Mummy she needed to wear her *buba*, *gele* and fineries, and come with me across town to Victoria Island that evening, to meet the difficult MD of BCCI, who thought I might be a fraud.

She did as was instructed; she was up-to-date with every aspect ofthe project, as she received daily briefings and progress reports. She waseven aware of the meeting I'd had at BCCI that morning.

We picked Ladi, my husband, up on the way; he'd agreed to come with us in spite of a nasty cold he was nursing. He knew the MD. They had once shared an office in Investment House where Ladi was working with the law firm, David Garrick and Co. Raza and Co. was applying fora Nigerian banking licence at the time.

Mummy had some choice words for the fellow during our mad dash to Victoria Island.

We arrived at his house and were met by his stunningly beautiful wife with her pale, flawless skin, and daughter, who, to my surprise, turned out to be someone I knew. She had also attended the University of Lagos.

They left us to talk, and I ran through the project methodically— the financing plan and the various lenders in the consortium. Ladichipped in with his in-depth legal expertise on the consortium loan, which was secured by the trust deed, with UBA Trustees as trustees to the consortium.

But Raza was still unmoved.

"Sammie should never have committed us to a building project inthe first place," he said. "He should know that we only offer loans with a maximum term of six months."

My mother watched as I began to marshal every argument I had left before she stopped me by whispering to me in Yoruba, "Taiwo, let'sgo. This is a waste of time."

In the car ride back to our respective homes, she thoroughly abused him. "Fool! Idiot!" Even going as far as using a Yoruba proverb: *Ni tori afeje eran, ka ma pe malu ni broda*[3]. She hissed. You could always count on my mother to use the aptcst Yoruba proverb relevant to a situation.

Fortunately, and not a second too soon, we were able to convince African Alliance, who had committed to the debenture in the sum of One Million Naira (₦1,000,000), to take up the shortfall created by BCCI in the bridge.

We were, therefore, able to hold our completion board meeting with the bridge and long-term lenders as planned, UBA acting as trustees to the loan and debenture stock, First Bank of Nigeria appointed custodian bank—an unusual nomenclature but very apt, their role wasto coordinate the consortium of lenders, call for funding as and when required throughout the project.

To my delight, less than a year later, BCCI completely collapsed.It turned out there was indeed something extremely dubious about this bank, funded with Arab money and managed by Pakistani bankers.

Bank of Crooks and Criminals Incorporated was its new nickname. It was exposed to have been nothing more than an avenuefor money laundering, round-tripping, recycling drug money and funds,and other nefarious transactions with dodgy characters and corporationsworldwide.

It now made sense why they did not, indeed, could not lend morethan six months of financing. It collapsed like a pack of cards, its license revoked worldwide. As it turned out, it actually did not have a banking license in many western countries. So many people lost money through them, and a number of their top officials went to jail.

It never ceases to amaze me how many people fall regularly for these fraudulent banking schemes, even though at least every decade or two, another major collapse occurs.

FUNDING THE CONSTRUCTION

The day before the scheduled completion board meeting, my motherinformed me that my siblings had requested a family meeting.

I'd been so engrossed with the crazy pace and maddening ups and downs of trying to raise long-term financing for the project, that I was completely blindsided by this meeting. I hadn't the slightest idea what it was about.

I was taken aback when my youngest sister, with whom I had always had a special bond and had always somehow felt protective towards, whispered to me just before the meeting started, "You know thismeeting is all about you, don't you?"

What?! She might as well have knocked me off my chair.

As I soon gathered, there had been a plot afoot; chattering, whisperings, and meetings amongst our siblings. So she told me.

My mother summoned us all to her study downstairs. Having crammed us in there, she asked the two protagonists to speak.

Their issue? I, Taiwo, was not the eldest, so why had I been giventhe huge task of raising the funds for Elephant House? They stated that the money could never be raised anyway, and concluded that our father had built eight blocks of six-unit apartments on the estate, in additionto the thirteen bungalows. We were eight children, and logically, his aimmust have been to divide the eight blocks amongst us. Now was the timeto do it.

---

3. *Because we want to eat steak, is that why we should call a cow 'Daddy! Mummy!'?*

My mother was as flabbergasted as I was.

"Who came up with this idea?" she'd asked incredulously.

Like all plots planned with malicious intentions, finger-pointing ensued.

It wasn't me! It was her!

Oh no! It wasn't me; you put me up to it!

…and on and on it went.

After shutting everybody up, my mother proceeded to explainthe shareholding structure of the company to us. The shares of Shonny Investments and Properties Company, she explained, was equally owned by our father and her. According to the terms of his will, he transferred 40% of his shares to her, releasing 10% of his remaining shares to his eight children, which meant she owned 90% of the company.

She made it very clear she had the power and prerogative to do whatever she liked with her company.

My mother had asked me to bring the loan and debenture loan stock agreements for Elephant House to the meeting. I hadn't understoodwhy she'd made this request, but now it was obvious I would have to show my siblings I was on top of matters regarding the project. I passed the documents around for everyone to assess for themselves. It was proofthat, despite the odds, I had successfully raised both the bridge and long-term loans for Elephant House, and confirmed that the completion board meeting would take place the next day.

Did I receive any congratulations, or a ‘Well done, Taiwo!’ from any of my siblings? Frankly, I don’t remember; it was a jarring experience, having my family gang up against me. Although this ambush, this betrayal, happened some thirty-seven years ago, I have never truly recovered from it, and I’m not sure I ever will.

But I really couldn’t dwell on it for long; I had to get prepared forthe very important completion board meeting for the project’s loan and debenture stock.

OPENING THE BID

And the Winner is...

Before opening the bid, Alan insisted we hold a meeting to review the design and ensure the project was as cost-efficient and as viable as possible.

Our architect was not at all pleased.

Who is Alan to mess with MY design? was his attitude.

Alan called me aside and emphasised that it was a speculative development with one single objective—making money for the company once the project is completed. It wasn't about the architect's ego, or that of anyone else for that matter.

"This is not some Chase Manhattan headquarters in New York,or some UN headquarters with the sole aim of showing how big and rich and excessive you are," he cautioned. "If your architect wants todo that, let him go fund his own project and indulge his ego as muchas he desires!" He continued, "We are going to be very practical andgo through this design, indeed this project, with one singular mindset—how will this design idea increase value, and thus, boost our rent? If theanswer to that question is it won't, we cut it out. If the answer is yes, weadd it in."

I was in 100% agreement.

With this objective in mind, we reviewed the potential lettable floor areas, and at Alan's insistence, we eliminated balconies on two upper floors which made no sense, literally led nowhere, and were not reachable. Nor did they serve any practical function as, say, space for plants or machinery. Through this methodical and meticulous processof assessing each design item, Alan came up with his *coup de grâce*—the introduction of a car lift into the development.

It would eliminate ramps, and it was an idea he had been toying with for a while, observing the enormous amount of lettable space wasted on high-rises by the installation of ramps which lead to the upperfloor car parks. In his estimation, those ramps eliminated, on average, two floors of valuable lettable space. He also argued that ramps—with their obligatory steep entrances into car parks—made it difficult for carsto manoeuvre onto them, forcing approaches to them to be a slow and stealthy process, which often led to a build-up of traffic at the entrancesto car parks in high-rises.

We did our due diligence, considering the viability of introducinga car lift into the design of Elephant House, and ultimately, agreed togo with it. The concept was entirely Alan Shelley's, but in his usual self-effacing manner, he never beat his chest about it.

As we set off to include the car lift in the design, we had no idea it would be the very first in Africa!

My Amazing Mother, Chief Mrs AliceOlaperi Shonibare (Née Olukoya)

My Father, Chief Samuel Olatunbosun Shonibare

Mum and Dad on their Wedding Day

My Young Self

My Young Self at Maryland Villa

Kensington Court Place, London, UK

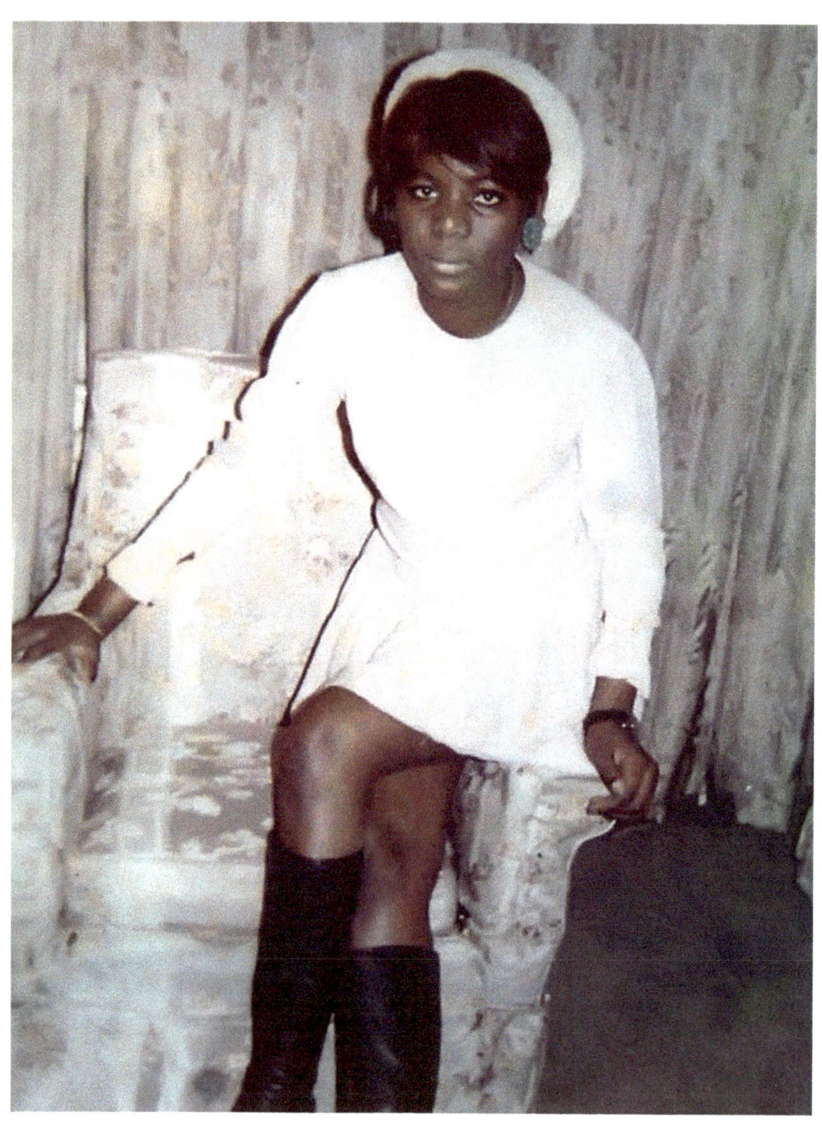

My Young Self at 21 Kensington Court Garden

Chief and Chief Mrs Shonibare

Lord Roy Thomson of Fleet Street

My Graduation from the University ofLagos, in 1973

Young Ladi Taiwo

Ladi and I in the Early Days

With my Twin Sister, Dr Mrs K.O. Dina, andOur Mother

My Late Brother, Gbeyintehinse Shonibare, with Our Mother, at the Opening Reception of the Elephant House Building on 17 January 1985

Elephant House on Broad Street

The Reception Area of Elephant House

At the Roof Top of Elephant House

Africa's First Car Lift, at Elephant House

The Car Lift Landing of Elephant House

My London Residence: Furniture Designedby Troloppe, and Made in Nigeria

Furniture Made by Troloppe in Lagos, andExported to my House in London

The Founding Chairman at the Atlantic Hall EducationalTrust Council's Inaugural Dinner in 1986

With Chief C.O. Ogunbanjo at the Atlantic HallEducational Trust Council's Inaugural Dinner

With Chief and Chief Mrs Ogunbanjo atthe Inaugural Dinner

Atlantic Hall School at its Temporary Site(Maryland Hotel)

Atlantic Hall's Administrative Office Block atthe Permanent Site in Poka Village, Epe

The Entrance Driveway to Atlantic Hall's Permanent Site

MOVING TO SITE

Looking back, and after years of being involved in several more projects following the Elephant House, I must say that our architectwas given an extraordinary free hand.

My mother, who was infinitely more conversant with such projects, even if only through her close partnership with my father and his multiple developments of major high-rises as Managing Director of NIPC, choseto leave all the decision-making, including the selection of the main contractor, to Modular Group, our architects. Amazingly, Lai Balogun and our project architects were left to pretty much do as they pleased; it'squite possible that in that era, it was the norm to have such unequivocal trust in your consultant. To be fair, by and large, they got the job done.

I must say though, I would never handle a project, even a much smaller one, that way again, nor would I recommend the architect be given such a degree of latitude.

We were informed that only five contractors working in Nigeria had the competence to handle such a complex and sophisticated project at the time: Julius Berger, Cappa & D'Alberto, G. Cappa, DTV, and Bouygues.

Bouygues was new in Nigeria, and we were told, had only completed one job, the four-storey UBA office block on part of the site of St Paul's Breadfruit Church. This should have been a red flag. The innocence of youth! Now, with years of experience behind me, I would have been extremely suspicious knowing they'd only worked on just theone project.

Everyone on our team was extremely impressed at the speed in which they had completed the job; they were clearly a favourite. To be honest, on a cursory visit to their flagship project for UBA at St Paul's Breadfruit Church, I was not that impressed with the finishing of the building. It seemed pretty shoddy to me, but *eh bien!*

At some point, I was introduced to Mr Laz, an ebullient French man, a master marketer who was in Nigeria to quickly accelerate the *entrée* of Bouygues into the Nigerian market, and secure major contractsfor the company.

The opening of the bid was a perfunctory affair. Bouygues had thebest price and won the contract.

To celebrate, we had a luncheon party at the Maryland Villa, my parent's lovely home in Shonibare Estate. We'd continued to refer to the mansion by that name, despite the catty remarks of an in-law who married into our family and chose to call it 'the so-called villa'!

It was a lovely Sunday dinner, a feast Henry VIII would have been proud of.

It was a family tradition for all of us to congregate at Mummy's house for Sunday lunch. The food was always delicious, and the conversations, fascinating. In a family where everyone held very strong opinions, and as this was before the invention of Google which would have quickly put to rest many of the long-protracted arguments we had, it's not hard to imagine how spirited those discussions were.

On this very special occasion, we were celebrating the fact that after twelve gruelling years—ten of obtaining the necessary approvals, two excruciating years of raising the required finance—the Elephant House project was finally a reality.

The lunch featured the continental menus from our La Parisienne restaurant next door, a long buffet table with an assortment of delicious Nigerian dishes and choice French wines. Naturally, champagne bottles were popped throughout.

In addition to Mr Laz, the Bouygues team included its young MD, Alain Richet, and equally young General Manager, Mr Replumaz. They were awestruck that I spoke fluent, if rather rusty, French.

A francophone client in Nigeria! They hadn't anticipated that, but were clearly delighted. They eagerly welcomed me into the inner circle of the French community in Lagos. I was shocked to discover they lived parallel French lives right there.

Their dinner parties would include French delicacies flown in thatvery evening on the UTA flight from Paris—like *escargots* and *foie gras*. They wouldn't, even out of curiosity, explore some of the great local fish that abound in the Lagos lagoon three quarters surrounded by the Atlantic Ocean. Instead, they would bring in fine French poisons, their *amends*, their *agile de mar barque*[4]. The lot.

Those dinners were always terribly enjoyable, with an abundanceof gastronomic delights. Although on one particular evening, I felt they had gone overboard. They brought in an accordion player to play Frenchfolk songs, the evening ending with everyone singing *La Marseillaise*. I'd felt like shouting, "Vive la France!"

The project commenced, and I was so terribly excited. I felt privileged tobe part of that dynamic group. Steve Mayaki, a representative of KFR, our project managers, was young, confident, and utterly professional. He was a qualified engineer from Loughborough University, and he'd had his professional training as an estate surveyor, with Knight Frank &Rutley, primarily in their London office. I listened intently to all his ideas, proposals, and recommendations for the project, and learnt a lot from him.

We held regular, sometimes daily, discussions. I gained tremendous knowledge and understanding of the requirements of project management, especially for a project of the magnitude of Elephant House.

I tracked my cash flow relentlessly and decided it was best we opena savings account into which we would make monthly contributions from cash flow generated mainly from Maryland Hotel.

4. *Rare regional French fish*

I made the decision based on a basic and clear understanding thatwe should always be ready to pay the interest on the loans, as and when required.

The project rolled on pretty much swiftly and smoothly after this,but for one hitch. Per the terms of the loan agreement, payments to the project would be triggered with a valuation from the quantity surveyors,which would be followed by the issuance of an Architect Certificate, and concluded by a request from the Project Manager to the custodian bank, First Bank of Nigeria, to obtain the prorated contribution of each one of the consortia of bridge financiers.

I received a call from the head of corporate finance of FBN.

"Why are you giving me all this work?" he asked, not masking his irritation. "I'd expected you to draw down the entire funds for the project in one scoop!"

"Are you kidding me?" I asked him. "Are you telling me you never understood the financial plan, the cash flows of the project which you financed, and of which you are a custodian bank?

The construction is expected to take fifty-six months! If we drew down the whole debt at the beginning of the project, the whole project would go belly up. How would you even know that we had not diverted the money to fund another project?"

His answer?

"You mean I am going to be called upon for the next three years to make a call on the other members of the consortium, requesting for their contributions periodically! If I had known that, I would certainly have charged you a whole lot more for playing that role."

It is a matter of record that not once throughout the four-year project did any of our bankers attend a site meeting.

When I'd queried one of them about this, it almost hurt that they took such little interest in the project we were working so hard to executewith textbook professionalism. The banker had informed me our projectwas on Broad Street, right next to their offices, which meant they wouldbe able to see it going up.

"Do you know how many billions we've loaned for projects in Kano, Maiduguri, Port Harcourt, where we have no clue of the veracity or otherwise of the report they send us?" he asked.

Goodness! It's all the more surprising banks didn't collapse in a sea of bad debts much earlier. I would like to think bankers have become infinitely more professional now; in fact, I am quite sure they have a much better understanding of finance for building development. They have, if anything, become ridiculously rigid.

After my conversation with the head of corporate finance, the project moved along in a very professional manner. Our guiding principle was straight out of Alan Shelley's playbook: how will a design or construction idea maximise our rent? If the answer was in the negative, we would cut it out of our building plans. If the answer was positive, wewould make sure to execute it.

We spent a lot of time debating and brainstorming on, for example, the issue of central air-conditioning which was notorious for the perennial problems they posed at that time for properties in which they were installed.

In the end, we decided to install floor by floor central air-conditioning units, instead of one large unit for the entire structure. The latter was the traditional way of installing them, a system proven to be unsatisfactory as evidenced by the many broken-down central air-conditioning systems in several high-rises throughout the city.

We installed one 40-horsepower unit on the ground and mezzanine floors; two independent 30-horsepower units for the 4th to 15th floors, and two independent 30-horsepower units on the 16th and 17th floors.

Our brand of choice for all units was the YORK® Air-conditioning Systems, relatively new in Nigeria at that time. York was reputed for its superior technology, and for providing efficient air quality solutions for homes across America. We were convinced that this American-made air-conditioning system had to be better than the carrier systems that were the vogue in Nigeria at the time.

Finally, the shell of the building was completed; all the subcontracts— mechanical and electrical—had been awarded, and good progress was being made on the installation of the passenger and car lifts.

Most importantly, we had kept to our timelines. I had already started putting pressure on Knight Frank & Rutley, who, in addition to being project managers, were also sole letting agents, to secure the one-year rent in advance on all the floors as they had committed to in the feasibility studies and as per their cash flow projections.

Sadly, my mentor, Alan Shelley, had left Nigeria in the middleof our project. Alan always had a perfect sense of timing, having lived in Nigeria for decades, cutting his tooth in the property market, and acquiring an unrivalled reputation as the ultimate dealmaker.

He was acutely aware that with the obligatory indigenisation of banks, financial institutions and many other foreign-owned corporate entities, the era in which he could package a development transaction in Nigeria over lunch with his mates, say, the Managing Director of Barclays Bank, or Standard Bank, or UBA or IBWA, was over.

Sadly, the effect of the indigenisation, with the government acquiring majority stakes in these institutions, was the politicisation of every one of them. With every change of government, a frantic hustle would ensue—curricula vitae would be flying all over town, with everyone jostling over who they could find with leverage in the new dispensation.

It would culminate with the dreaded announcement, the immediate dissolution of the boards of all banks! This would be followed, a few weeks later, by fresh appointments of those with leverage, people within the new government.

This, tragically, led to the gradual erosion of professionalism in these institutions, and the general fall in standards in many of them, sometimes, irreversibly so.

Whatever you might say about Alan, he would never put his signature on a project which he was not certain was backed by the relevant data supporting the investment in the project.

Alan, who was known to smoke a pipe, was adept at meticulously rolling the tobacco, cleaning the pipe, and taking his time ensuring it was just right. While undergoing this laborious process, he would consider a proposition in his head, carefully pondering various viable options, and finally, as he blew out the smoke, he'd somehow come up with the perfect solution to whatever he had been contemplating. That I was once told by one of his colleagues.

He never promoted a project that did not succeed. Sadly, after leaving Nigeria halfway through our project, Alan, despite all his remarkable talents, was not so clever at selecting a good successor.

The directors at Knight Frank & Rutley (KFR) rustled througha couple of letters of intent and commitment from off-takers they had secured years earlier, only to hit a dead end—not one single institution that had written a letter of commitment to take up space when the building was constructed up to the top floor and had promised to pay theagreed rent one year in advance, fulfilled their commitment. Not one.

I argued passionately with the KFR director, even threatening to sue the agency for dropping the ball. I argued that the whole projectwas predicated on the assumption and commitment that these off- takers would be ready, once the top floor had been reached, to make the necessary, agreed-upon rent payments.

Alas, the reality was that I was the one who had to deal with the looming terror of multiple defaults to contractors and banks for loan interest payments.

I made up my mind that day, I would never again put my fate in the hands of consultants. To this day, I have always had a healthy dose of slight scepticism in swallowing expert consultant advice, hook, line, and sinker, without at least seeking second opinions.

I needed to think quickly on my feet and come up with a new strategy, just as we had done when raising the long-term loan for the project; I did not have a minute to waste.

I decided to start with first finding tenants for the ground and mezzanine floors, which, it occurred to me, would be an ideal location for a banking hall.

Researching various banks, to find ones with poorly located headquarters, I decided my line of attack would be to attract these banks to the newly minted Elephant House.

Eventually, I found one—Bank of India. It was located in a tiny space off Breadfruit Street, on Daramola Street, amid the crowded market of Lagos Island. It shared its banking hall—for goodness sakes!— with a Bata Shoes shop. I climbed up their rickety staircase and met theirManaging Director, a lovely man called Mukhtar Bello, truly one of the finest human beings I have ever come across. He was kind, earnest, gentle, and unusually frank for a banker. That meeting was the beginningof a long and enduring friendship.

He confirmed the intention of their bank to raise their profile, andhow desperate they were to move out of their unsuitable office space to afirst-class office accommodation such as Elephant House.

We were able to strike an agreement on the spot for the lease of the ground and mezzanine floors of Elephant House to Bank of India, soon to be renamed Allied Bank, with the completion of the indigenisation and the acquisition of majority shares of the bank by the Federal Government.

We also agreed that they would lease the 15th and 16th floors for their head office.

I was equally blunt with him. The project was on track to be completed as per projected timelines, but we had run into cash flow problems because of the failure of our letting agents to secure tenants for all the floors as we reached the last floor as undertaken by them. We needed the Bank of India to pay rent for the four floors, three years in advance, to enable us to complete the project by the stipulated time.

Amazingly, he agreed to these terms and followed this up by paying us the agreed rents for four floors, three years in advance.

I left his office with a hop and jiggle. This was a reaffirmation that if we wanted to let our seventeen floors, I needed to be personally involved. Period.

With the injection of this additional capital, we were ableto advance the project, but the slowdown which this delay caused significantly affected the cost of the project. We clearly needed to go back to our bridge lenders and apply for additional funding.

I really do hate borrowing; I doubt anyone enjoys it. Nevertheless,I had to face these bankers, some of whom were arrogant, and request additional financing. Thankfully, we were able to raise the needed capital from our three main bridge financiers—First Bank, UBA, and with great reluctance, IBWA. How can I ever forget the rudeness and affront of the French director of IBWA, who, meeting me at a cocktail party at the French Commercial Attaché's residence, proceeded to openly discuss our project in front of everyone at the party!

"Left to me, I would never have invested in that project. It's not right at the centre of Broad Street; I don't see how you will be able to letit," he'd said with contempt.

I gave him an appropriate, rude response and walked away, gratified that I'd given him a piece of my mind. What a cheeky fellow!

It was, however, not so funny that he raised the topic about my, ashe saw it, 'lack of respect' for IBWA during a credit committee meeting.In the small milieu that was the finance community, it got back to me that IBWA was reluctant to join the other two banks in the consortium of First Bank and UBA to finance the shortfall in capital needed to complete Elephant House because I had been rude to their French Executive Director!

I was flabbergasted and quickly set up a meeting with the Managing Director of IBWA, Mr Olashore. He was a seasoned banker and a very urbane gentleman.

I met Mr Olashore at the IBWA office and explained the circumstances of my meeting with the French Executive Director and the nature of our conversation, including my retort to his cheekiness. AsI recounted what had transpired, I could sense that he was a bit amused.

However, he did try to articulate a defence of the French director, albeit a weak one, that it was just a misunderstanding, adding that the director actually happened to be married to a Nigerian, although Icouldn't quite figure out what this revelation had to do with anything!

In any event, I was able to finalise the refinancing with all three banks participating in the consortium and the project was back on track.

It was at this stage of the project that I became pregnant with my last born, but I was determined to keep going for as long as I could, focusedon making sure that the project continued as seamlessly as possible.

I hid the discomfort of my morning sickness from the rest of the team, which seemed worse than it had been during my previous pregnancies. Most days, I was extremely tired, but I did not let this interfere with fulfilling my various roles and meeting my commitments. I even remember getting on the external makeshift lift, pregnant, to access the upper floors, despite my fear of heights.

The last stage of the project involved leasing 10,000 square metresof vacant office space. Alan Shelley had been right when he'd cautionedme that letting 10,000 square metres of commercial office space would not be an easy task. But failure was not an option. I simply had to pull allthe stops to let those darned floors!

We received assistance from an unexpected source, our contractor, Bouygues. Their finance director at the time was a former top management staff of Commercial Bank Credit Lyonnais (CBCL), who had just obtained a banking licence in Nigeria at the time, with the provision that they had to start operations within months.

Having concluded on leasing the ground floor of the moderately-sized SCOA building, which had been recently completed and was located directly opposite Elephant House, they were easily convinced tolease the 5th and 6th floors of Elephant House as their new headquarters.

We approached the methodology of how we would set up the head office of a prestigious bank, such as Commercial Bank Credit Lyonnais, in a building that was six months, at least, from being commissioned, and with such essential services as lifts, sewage treatment and generators not quite in place yet, in a very pragmatic manner.

I must say that Bouygues had some of the shrewdest and smartest engineers I have ever met, who came up with some truly ingenious solutions. They would manage all service aspects of the property for CBCL until the official handover.

As far as I am aware, this was their first foray into facilities management, but it does not surprise me that they subsequently developed this arm of their business, becoming one of the biggest and most respected real estate management companies in the world today.

They installed a generator with the capacity to power two floors and one lift. Working with office interior designers, they quickly outfitted the two floors of CBCL to first-class standards.

The Bouygues team managed to implement a system for eliminating waste generated from these two floors, before the commissioning of the sewage treatment plant.

Their solution for the lift was hilarious. At this stage, testing of the four-passenger lifts was in full swing, however, it would be a while before they could be officially launched. Bouygues took over one lift that was virtually ready, except for the fact that the computer commands to call the lifts up or down were not yet installed.

They engaged two lift attendants, one inside and the other on the ground floor, and equipped each with a bugle. Yes, you read that right. A bugle! They would sound loud to call the lifts up and down.

Very quaint, very practical, very effective.

Alhaji Mukhtar Bello, the Managing Director of Bank of India was proven right in deciding to commit to leasing the ground and mezzanine floors. As the building neared completion, I was able to convince him to move all their operations to Elephant House; they ended up leasing five additional floors.

Finishing cost a fortune. It was relatively easy building two floors at a time every month, especially once we got into the groove of it. Coming down to do the finishing was another matter altogether, the associated costs were brutal on one's cash flow. We simply had no choice but to lease the remaining floors.

I approached the Managing Director of United Bank of Africa, Alhaji Mutallab Bello. UBA had been one of our main financiers, a partof the consortium of bridge financiers, whilst UBA Trustees were the trustees to the debenture stock.

Word was out that UBA was thoroughly fed up with their leaseof numerous floors of NIDB which had, as a result of poor facility management, quickly fallen into disrepair.

I arranged a meeting with him, armed with the knowledge that they required a suitable space for the bank, and earnestly explained the problem we were facing. I reminded him that they were our bankers andlet him know just how much we owed them. I made my pitch: we neededUBA to lease our vacant floors and relocate their large office from the NIDB to Elephant House so that we could use the funds to repay their loans. I shall never forget his response.

"Mrs Taiwo, if I go about renting properties from all the companiesI have loaned money to, what kind of banker would I be?"

I didn't miss a beat. "But Alhaji, perhaps your other borrowers have alternative sources to repay their debt. We don't. It's the smart thingto do," I said, tongue in cheek.

He laughed heartily.

That was how UBA leased five floors from our list of vacant floors. I was not done yet. I had discovered a winning strategy, and so

I approached First Bank, another lender for the project, offering them the unique opportunity of leasing space in this ultra-modern building, which had been carefully selected for a range of commercial, investment, and merchant banks only. In this era, banks, unlike the practise today, were able to determine their area of specialty, based on the value of their shareholdings, amongst other factors, and in effect determine the clientele which best suited their area of expertise.

They took the bait and leased one floor for their data processing headquarters.

I did it! How on earth did I find a way over of what had seemed an insurmountable mountain? I truly believe it was by the grace of God.

I was now seven-and-a-half months pregnant. We'd made a last-minute addition to the building's design, a penthouse, that would entail the creation of an 18th floor. I was eager to see how it turned out.

I walked—yes, walked—eighteen floors, seven-and-a-half months pregnant, up the flight of stairs (the external temporary lift had long been removed), and saw the penthouse in all its splendour, satisfied and reassured that not only was the funding to complete the project fully in place, but the construction and finishing also was in the hands of our very competent contractors, Bouygues, and a generally professional team of consultants. Through sheer grit and the awesome blessing and grace of God, I had successfully leased out virtually all the vacant space in this enormous building, before completion, to four prestigious banks: Commercial Bank Credit Lyonnais, Allied Bank, United Bank of Africa, and First Bank. I managed this completely on my own; not a penny was paid to any leasing agent for letting fees.

I felt I deserved and had earned some time off so I headed to London, in preparation for the delivery of my baby, a son, Leye, who arrived a few weeks later on 19 March 1983.

Our family was now complete with the addition of my baby boy; we now had two boys and one girl. I was ecstatic. *My cup runneth over*.

I spent the next couple of months in London, without a care in the world, embracing the joys of motherhood, and enduring the hard slug of getting my body back in shape. For the first time in years, I did not worry or give any thought to Elephant House, Maryland Hotel, or the other subsidiaries of the company where I served on the board.

While I loved every minute of it, after three months of taking care of my baby and going to the gym every day, I was ready to return home and get back to work. I discovered that I actually enjoyed, and hadmissed, the thrilling and fast-paced world of business.

Elephant House was, at last, nearing completion, I was beside myselfwith excitement.

I couldn't wait to actually experience the electrification of the building, to witness the lights coming on and seeing all eighteen floors lit up, and adding our light to the skylight of Lagos.

I was shocked to discover that the electrical consultant who had designed the electrical installation of this landmark project did notshare my enthusiasm. While I raced to witness the electrification of the building, which was to be done gradually, from bottom to top floor, our electrical consultant and designer were nowhere to be found! I suspectedthat perhaps he was actually terrified that the electrification could go horribly wrong.

I was disappointed he didn't have confidence in his own design. I mean, really!

Thankfully, it went on without a glitch.

MANAGING ELEPHANT HOUSE

The plan was to have the property management division of Knight Frank & Rutley (KFR) take over the management of the building once completed. True, they had failed spectacularly as letting agents, but they had been excellent project managers.

We were completely blindsided, however, when UBA—one of our anchor tenants—insisted that they did not want Knight Frank & Rutley to be the building's managers. They were relocating most of their key departments from the NIDB building down the road to Elephant House; the appalling management at NIDB was being carried out by KFR's facility management division. They insisted that they were not going to go through that nightmare again.

Instead, they wanted hands-on management of the facilities by the owners. I guess having worked with us through the process of raising the finance, and witnessing the progress of the construction and its completion within four-and-a-half years (record time, it has to be said, despite my disappointment that we did not complete the project within three-and-a-half years as projected), and observing my tenacity in singlehandedly finding tenants for the building, they were confident that we would establish a first-class facility management for the building, once we put our minds to it.

They were eager to avoid a situation where a management team would supposedly be in situ, but effectively the person on site would be a relatively junior facility manager with no real authority to make critical decisions for the building when necessary. The consequence of this could be disastrous for the tenants, who would have to wait weeks and sometimes months for repairs to be made.

Although I had managed the 60-bed Maryland Hotel for over twelve years, I wasn't sure I wanted to take on the management of a sophisticated eighteen-storey, 65,000 square metres of an ultra-modern office block comprising complex equipment including a car lift!

As I always did, I discussed the issue with my mum, and, God bless her, she had no doubt that I was perfectly capable of handlingthis monumental task. She'd had her own disastrous experience with 'professional' facility managers, who originally managed our Maryland residential estate. Mum had some choice words for them, reminding me that she had ultimately sacked them and set up our own facility management department to take care of the estate.

I worked with Steve Mayaki, with whom I had worked closely in the project management of Elephant House, and in my opinion—as I told Alan Shelley on the regular occasions we met up in London—shouldhave been made partner in Knight Frank & Rutley when he was leaving.Steve developed a facility management blueprint for Elephant House, helped recruit key staff, and agreed to be our consultant for, at least, thefirst year.

I had one request: that we bring Popo from the estate to work at Elephant House; in fact, I insisted on this.

Popo was quite the character; clean-shaven, always in dark sunglasses, day or night. He truly looked like the quintessential mafia thug! I suspect wearing the sunglasses was a strategy to hide the fact that he was barely literate. Nevertheless, he was, undoubtedly, one of the best electricians I had ever met. He was also unflinchingly loyal.

We had been wise enough to bring him over to Elephant Housea good six months before the completion of the project to shadow the electrical contractor as his team installed the building's electrical system. He had grasped it all, understanding the nuts and bolts of the most sophisticated electrical installation.

I gave him an additional role as a janitor; he was also, informally,our ears and eyes in the neighbourhood. I let him know that he must view Elephant House as his baby and that I counted on him to be my personal security on the beat.

The role fit him like a glove, and very quickly, everyone in the neighbourhood viewed him as somewhat of a mafia don in the area, albeit, a benign one.

I moved my office to Elephant House and was officially nominated Managing Director of Shonny Investments and Properties Company Limited. My mother, now barely sixty years old, had decided to retire from the company.

At Elephant House, I set up my office on the 17th floor; it was simply and beautifully decorated. My mother chose not to have an office at the headquarters, though we did have a large boardroom for meetings, which she would still preside over.

The official opening of Elephant House took place on 17 January 1984, the 20th anniversary of my father's death. My mother loved him until the day she died, and though he'd had nothing to do with the Elephant House project, she dedicated the building to him. Mum had acquired the land on which Elephant House is situated after his death and subsequently acquired three additional sites. After ten years of relentless pursuit of the necessary approval from the Lagos State Government, we had finally arrived at this important milestone.

All our consultants, the full force of the Bouygues management, family members, and their invited guests were in attendance. I was acutely conscious of potential sibling rivalries, triggered by the fact that I had, indeed, pulled this off, despite their reservations and lack of support.

There were no speeches that day, I made sure of that. I simply mingled with all the guests and members of my family, proud and extremely gratified that the project had been completed.

None of my siblings congratulated me or, at the very least, acknowledged my role in accomplishing this great feat. But it didn't matter; I was proud of all I'd overcome to get to this day, proud that, at long last, Elephant House was officially open.

CREATIVE JUICES

My dear friend, Nikue Akpe, is my go-to whenever I need a great book recommendation. He usually recommends books on a range of subjects including philosophy, psychology, and history. As an avid reader, I strongly believe in the transformative powerof books to expand one's mindset and worldview.

I read, in one of such books, that most of us only ever use 25% of our creative faculty, without ever exploring the other 75% while we're alive. What a colossal waste! It was truly eye-opening to learn that everyone has the capacity to be an artist, a musician, a philosopher, an entrepreneur, or a writer, but most of us are not curious enough to dive deeper to explore these endless possibilities. I made up my mind that I was going to follow my passions and use as many of my talents in this one lifetime as possible.

Completing the Elephant House at such a young age left me with severe withdrawal syndrome; for five years, I had been totally absorbed with the frenetic pace of the project—fraught, as it was, with myriad challenges. I was now Managing Director of Shonny Investments and Properties Company (SIPC), with specific responsibilities of facility management of the Elephant House building while managing the payback of loans taken out for the project. I had relinquished my role as Director of the Maryland Hotel to my youngest brother, Gbeyin, who had just obtained an MBA from the University of Nebraska in Omaha.

The completion of Elephant House also, in many ways, marked some new beginnings in my personal life. I completed my own maisonettes,two large developments in a lovely new neighbourhood, on land which had been generously and kindly given to each one of us by my mother.

I was able to leverage my new-found knowledge, proven aptitudefor raising capital, and solid relationships with a number of banks, to obtain a residential loan at the unheard-of rate of prime minus 3.5%.

I was informed by UBA representatives that I was the first non- staff member who had ever been granted this prudential loan. I found this to be a bit ridiculous as banks should have been encouraging the development of the mortgage market by facilitating, as much as possible,the release of funds needed by many Nigerians to build their own houses.

I made friends with Pamela Field, the lovely, energetic wife of David Field, the Managing Director of Seagram, who were clients of Ladi's law firm. Pam was American and taught at the Lebanese Community School. She was dynamic, adventurous, and great fun to be around; we clicked straight away.

It was Pamela who introduced me to the African Book Club, an eclectic group of women, mostly expatriates. They were typically part of the diplomatic, business, and finance communities in Lagos. We read books about Africa or by Africans, met weekly to discuss the book of the week, rotating the homes in which we met. Reading and reviewing a different book every week demanded a certain degree of discipline; there was no way to short circuit the process.

Our group held deep, philosophical discussions as we reviewed these books, and in the process gained incredible and valuable insights about life, love, friendship and so much more.

I made lifelong friends through the book club, including the ravishingly beautiful May El Khalil, founder of the NGO, Lebanese Ladies in Nigeria which grants scholarships to deserving youths; and the statuesque Scottish artist, Ella Johnson. Ella had an interesting background. Her father had been one of the first professors of medicine at the University College Hospital, Ibadan, and she had attended secondary school at St Anne's School for Girls in Ibadan. There was the erudite Chitra, from India, who had a lovely husband; they were passionately in love with each other, which was fascinating to me as I learned that theirs had been an arranged marriage. I gathered that many Indian mothers were good at selecting the right partners for their children, which is whymany arranged marriages were successful.

I thoroughly enjoyed being in the company of these interesting and charming ladies and very much looked forward to our weekly Thursday meetings. Besides one very pushy member, who was forever trying to sell us one product or the other, I got along effortlessly with the rest of the group and learned so much from them.

I was introduced to the rhythmic style of the incomparable Maya Angelou. Her autobiographical, *I Know Why the Caged Bird Sings* transported me to another world entirely. I found myself thinking about scenes from the book at the oddest of times.

Karen Blixen's *Out of Africa* was simply riveting; our reviewer was the Danish ambassador to Nigeria, who gave us an extraordinary ringside view and insider knowledge of the backstory of the life and times ofKaren Blixen in Denmark.

I loved the novels of Buchi Emecheta; her writing style was conversational, unpretentious, and effective.

Till today, I cherish the memories of my time with the ladies of the African Book Club. I particularly loved how deeply we dared to delveinto the deepest and most sensitive parts of our souls during our weeklybook review discussions. The book club allowed me to decompress from juggling various business ventures, to fully indulge in my passion for literature.

It was around this time that Ladi and I moved into our lovely new home,situated on half an acre in Ikeja GRA. Moving to a brand-new space offered me another opportunity to explore my creativity; this time, my artistic skills of interior designing.

I have always loved the grand curtains featured in many period movies like *Gone with the Wind*. I can't count the number of times I have watched this movie. Of course, it is very much a movie of its time, so I do put some of the racially insensitive scenes in context. However, in termsof storytelling, universal themes explored production design, and how well put together it is, in my opinion no greater film has ever been made.

I was fascinated by the beautiful, grand homes in the movie, withthe fabulous furnishing and grand curtains with elegant swags and tails. Inspired by this, I knew exactly how I would decorate our lovely new home: pastel-coloured chintz, with white rattan, lots of indoor plants and stunning curtains, pinch pleats with simple swags and tails in the main living room, Austrian blinds in the dining rooms and Roman blinds in the bathrooms.

I soon discovered that I had a major problem: no one in Nigeria made these types of curtains at the time. I made a lot of inquiries and eventually, through a friend, I was connected with an enterprising youngAmerican woman, married to a Nigerian, who could make Austrianand Roman blinds. Making the curtains was more a hobby for her thana business venture. I commissioned her to make Austrian and Roman blinds for our new home, which I was very pleased with; they fit perfectlyover our French windows and helped create the precise ambiance I had wanted for our home.

Natural light filtered into the living room through the enormous French windows which were decorated with Austrian blinds in pastel colours; sofas covered in chintz prints; white rattan furniture with lots of large palms, ferns, and other indoor plants.

I was thrilled with my efforts and felt extremely blessed that this move coincided with my move to my penthouse office in the newly completed Elephant House. I felt nervous at this cornucopia of blessings, felt guilty almost, and somewhat apprehensive.

It occurred to me that the lady, aged beyond her years by the relentlessly hard life she must have been living, who eked out a living roasting plantain and groundnuts to sell at her illegal spot in front of Elephant House, must wonder how come she was so hard done by God. I wondered what she thought, seeing me arrive to work every day, perhaps assuming, erroneously, that young girl owned the enormous building. How could that be?

Those thoughts flashed through my mind on many occasions, andI felt a strong urge to do something about it. I called Popo, our janitor and chief electrician, to whom we had handed over the keys of ElephantHouse.

"Popo," I told him. "Please, let these hardworking women who hawk their goods by our office, know the extent of debt we are carryingfrom the construction of Elephant House. Explain to them that these debts rest on the shoulders of me, the young girl they see driving up to the office every day. If anything goes wrong, it is on her, her burden to bear. Ask them to pray for me, that I beg for their prayers, for I often layin bed at night worrying."

God bless Popo. He did as I'd asked and before I knew it, I had made allies in all the street traders around the building. I allowed them to continue their various enterprises—roasting plantain, selling peanuts and other goods—in a tiny corner by the building. I was one of their best customers. Nothing beats roasted plantain and peanuts for lunch!

Decorating my new home had given me tremendous pleasure; I found itto be a very satisfying experience. I decided that I was going to explore my creative side further by developing a cottage industry making curtains.

My mother had always kept tailors on her household staff. She loved sewing, buying exotic fabrics from all over the world, cutting and making them up into kaftans or the Yoruba traditional *iro* and *buba*. She had the tailor hem and stitch decorative pieces to them. It was a handy and practical addition to the staff. It is a rather Victorian thing to do, asit was common for a certain class of ladies in the Victorian era to have a seamstress as part of their household staff.

I started by practising with my mother's tailors. My innate skillas a keen and curious observer of people and my surroundings came in handy. I found myself examining curtains wherever I was in the world, taking note of how the swags were configured. I did this obsessively, andnot once did anyone question or stop me, no matter whether I was at a hotel, restaurant, or other public places.

My house served as a guinea pig as I would try out new curtain designs and drape concepts on our windows.

It didn't take long before friends commissioned me to designtheir homes. I set up a company for my interior design business called 'Troloppe'. Ladi had always been good at coming up with the perfect name for a company. He felt that the name, 'Troloppe', connoted the feeling of an old established company and figured that the 'T', sort of represented our surname, Taiwo.

Although I liked the name, there was something vaguely familiar about the word that made me uneasy. Sure enough, I looked it up in the dictionary and was aghast.

Trollop: a dirty filthy woman, the female version of a tramp

Goodness!

However, the more I thought about it, the more it grew on me, regardless of what the word actually meant. I decided to just go with it.

I was always taken aback that most of my clients wanted me to transform their homes with very little input from them. I couldn't get my head around allowing anyone such latitude with my home.

The first home I worked on, I received zero input from the client.

"Just do it the way you decorated your home," was my client's simple instruction.

After working in this manner a couple more times, I realised I didnot enjoy replicating the same décor over and over again. I forced my client's involvement.

Many people could not articulate what they liked or didn't like.It was surprising the number of people who did not know what their favourite colours were, or have a basic idea of their preferred decorating style.

"What is your favourite colour?" I would ask, with my colour chartin hand.

"Don't know!" was the typical client response.

I would then proceed with my time-tested method of eliminationin a quest to uncover my client's unconscious design preferences.

"Red?"

No.

"Blue?"

"Hmm…"

"Ok, midnight blue, sky blue, pastel…?"

"Oh! Come to think of it, I do love pastel blue."

"What about green?"

"Never!"

…and on and on it would go until, *Voila!* I would find a fitting colour scheme that matched the client's tastes.

I would show them various decorating styles, emphasising that thekey to great design is properly harmonising different elements; the yin and the yang, rhyme and rhythm. I encouraged them to throw one or twooriginal pieces in the mix to make a room really pop.

I grew this business from a cottage business with just three tailors to a small-scale business with twenty tailors, an installation team comprising carpenters, and Sunday, my outstanding upholstery expert.

Many of the staff were Togolese. They had the requisite training and patience to learn, on-the-job, new concepts, and techniques.

I also hired some marketing staff. They were effective in ensuringthat we had a presence in most furniture showrooms in Lagos at the time.We had an agent in the North who helped secure substantial contracts for enormous palatial homes across Nigeria, including Maiduguri, Oguta, Imo State, Jos, and Kano. This provided the perfect opportunity for me to finally travel across Nigeria, a dream I'd long held.

My first visit to Maiduguri was quite memorable. The direct, nonstop flight was just short of three hours. On arrival, I was surprised at how the people looked so different from any Nigerian I had met. Theywere not Fulani, neither were they Hausa, the predominant ethnic groupin the North; they were Kanuri, most of them tall and slender with very distinct tribal marks on their faces.

The heat was almost unbearable, the roads dusty and the streets bare; there was hardly anyone outside. I had never seen so many flies orinsects in my life, larger than any insect I had ever seen.

With the heat so severe, and after such a long, stressful journey,I had fancied a glass of cold beer once I got to my hotel room but was disappointed to find out that the hotel didn't serve alcohol. I was met by Mohammed, our agent in the Northern states, who proved invaluable to our business; I learned so much from him.

I was surprised by the ease at which people could travel from Maiduguri to Chad, a neighbouring country. It seemed there was barely a border dividing the two countries and minimal border control.

The contractor building the house we had been contracted to decorate was from Chad and spoke fluent French; he travelled back andforth across the border several times a day to pick up one thing or the other.

At some point during my trip, it occurred to me that I was far away from home, and I was reminded of my time, many years ago, in Penrhos College in North Wales. The Beach Boys' song, *I Want to Go Home*, played over and over in my head as I sat in my hotel room in Maiduguri.

In September 1995, I bought an apartment in London.

I quickly got to work designing the space. I visited many high- end furniture shops including Harrods and Maples. Instinctively, my eyes always fixated on the most unique designs; usually. Those exquisite and pricey pieces had cautionary signs placed in front of them:

DO NOT SIT

DO NOT TOUCH

DO NOT TAKE PICTURES

It was my son, Leye, who, after we had gone through yet another one of these shops, turned to me and said, "Mummy, they need a Troloppe in England." I thought it was an excellent idea, given the limited available options.

I conceptualised the design theme of the flat, got someone to takeall the relevant measurements, and came up with the colour scheme for the interior—black, white, and gold for the living room, pastel colours for the bedrooms, and white Austrian blinds with black hemmings for thedining room.

I was determined to execute the project to perfection. I envisageda future where I could possibly have a Troloppe in the UK, Europe, or elsewhere, in the future. Why not?

I would make all the curtains in Nigeria, create the unique pieces of furniture I had in mind—an empire sofa, two Egyptian occasional chairs, and another pair of ornate occasional chairs.

Most ambitious was my plan to build stunning and intricate twin display units. I had a very specific, unique design in my head. They would fit perfectly in the two recesses in the main sitting room.

Back in Lagos, I supervised the production of swags and tailsfor the living room's curtains, with exquisite trimmings and finishing; each curtain in the bedrooms was produced to the highest world-class standards, as were the Austrian blinds in the dining room.

I hired four artisans from various parts of the city to manufacture the furniture, and oversaw the entire process to ensure that they executedmy vision for the finished products. The artisans included a master sculptor, who carved beautiful lion heads for the twin, Egyptian-style occasional chairs; a carpenter who created the frames for the empire sofaand produced my *pièce de résistance*—the carefully designed twin display units for the living room.

I was particularly nervous about the display units, praying that I had the measurements just right, to ensure that they fit comfortably intothe intended space.

Then came the spray painter, who was tasked with achieving a lacquered look, to give the pieces that unique, special finish. He neededto have stencilling expertise as the finished product would feature a lineof gold-rimmed stencilling to offset the black lacquered finish.

Completing the process would be the upholstery, which wasrelatively easy as I had absolute confidence in my master upholster, Sunday, who was truly world-class.

In the end, the finished products were considerable in number. I inquired and found out I would need a 20-foot container on a cargo boatto transport everything to the UK. I promptly booked the container and made arrangements with the shippers. They were bemused as they had never heard of anyone carrying furniture from Nigeria to the UK.

It turned out it cost very little, definitely way less than I'd anticipated,to transport the furniture to the UK. The ship would set sail the first or second week in January 1996 arriving in Southampton within two weeks.The cargo was categorised as personal effects and would therefore not attract any duty tax.

I arrived in England that freezing cold February of 1996, excited and barely able to contain myself. The other pieces of furniture which we'd from stores in the UK, to complement our masterpieces from Nigeria, were only just arriving. There is a standard minimum of two tothree months' wait for delivery of furniture in most stores in the UK. A huge portion of them are imported from far and wide.

I was particularly excited that my mother was also in London, and when I told her that the container was arriving that February morning, she moved in with me from her own house to witness the process of everything coming together in my new flat. After what felt like forever, the long lorry with the shipped container finally roared into our street, taking up a huge chunk of it.

One by one the furniture, furnishings and curtains were brought in. We opened the boxes, tentatively and nervously, but there was reallyno reason for the nerves as everything looked fabulous! Most importantly,the display units fitted the recess snugly, just as I had planned. It was the perfect width and the perfect height for the flat's high ceiling.

My mother was impressed and bursting with pride.

"How do you do these things, my husband?" she asked, as she tookit all in.

We busied ourselves installing the curtains, with constant 'oohs' and 'ahhs coming from the installers.

"You made these in Africa? It would have cost a small fortune in England." They couldn't believe it.

While in London, my mother invited many of her friends over to that flat to "come and see what Taiwo had done!" It was gratifying to know how proud she was of me.

ESTABLISHING ATLANTIC HALL

In the 70s, I watched as, one by one, all my friends got married. By the end of that decade, I don't believe I had a single friend who wasn't married, had at least one baby, and had settled down, juggling both a professional career and married life.

The five of us girls—my twin sister, Kehinde, Eniola, Gbemi, Bisi, and myself—were close, maintaining daily contact, and sharing in each other's joys and woes. We decided we needed to set a day aside for just ourselves, to meet up and talk about any and everything. The kids and our respective husbands were not included in this meet-up. We would kick off our shoes, and most importantly, treat ourselves to a gastronomic feast.

We alternated hosting this intimate dinner and discussion at each other's homes. We would go through the effort of laying a beautiful table and having food fit for royalty prepared, engaging in spirited conversations throughout.

Though each one of us had different personalities, we were all well-read, curious, and aware of current local, national, and global events, which we discussed passionately. We were usually rather garrulous, and very opinionated in the most innocuous manner; after all, we were amongst our dearest and closest, and it was fine and safe to be totally uninhibited.

We talked about everything, sharing our views, often forcefully, but always left those get-togethers with deep love, a strengthened sisterlybond, and appreciation for one another. It never crossed anyone's mind then that our personalities might later clash and stoke the embers of hurtand distrust amongst us.

A topic that came up frequently at our meetups was the deteriorating state of secondary schools in Nigeria. As our children grew, nearing the age when they would take the common entrance exams for entry into secondary schools, the conversation inevitably centred on the arduous task of preparing our young children for those critical exams. Achievingthe best grades guaranteed admission into top schools like King's College and Queen's College.

We had already commenced the formidable preparation required for our children if they were to have a fighting chance of gaining admissions to those highly sought-after institutions. The odds wereheavily weighed against them, as the entrance into those schools was based on a quota system designed to weigh in favour of children whose parents came from the Northern states.

Before and after independence, Nigeria was a Federal state comprising three regions—the Northern, Western and Eastern Provinces. In 1963, two provinces were detached from the Western Region to form the new Mid-Western Region. In 1967, the regions were replaced with twelve states by a military decree; only the Mid-Western Region escaped division.

In 1976, several new states were created, making nineteen. From 1987 to 1991, the states were further subdivided to twenty-one states, and later, Abuja, the new Federal Capital Territory, was added. Between 1991 and 1996, additional states were added by further subdividing regions, with the country now having thirty-six states.

Northern states were considered educationally disadvantaged, which was why the quota system was weighted in their favour. Westerneducation in the old Western Region, and particularly in the coastal areasof Nigeria such as Calabar, was well ahead of the rest of Nigeria.

There were many historical reasons behind this gap in education between the west and other parts of the country. The end of the slave trade led to educated freed slaves from Sierra Leone making theirway to Lagos. On their journey, they converted many to the Christian faith, and engendered in them, respect and appreciation for western education. British missionaries followed closely after, also bringing with them western education, and establishing first-class missionary schools. The oldest university in West Africa, Fourah Bay College, a western-style university in the neighbourhood of Mount Aureole in Freetown, Sierra Leone, was founded on 18 February 1827. It was formally affiliated with Durham University from 1876 to 1967. Christopher Sapara Williams CMG was the first indigenous lawyer. He was called to the English bar on 17 November 1879. These factors contributed to the tremendous gapin education between indigenes of the old Western Region and the rest of Nigeria.

I didn't think it was fair that descendants from this region should have to pay for the educational gap in the form of the quota system. Families from areas of the country not favoured by this system had to double their efforts and ensure their children would be ready to more than excel in the common entrance exams to guarantee their entry intothe best schools.

Our children typically started preparation for the exams from the age of seven. After a full day at school, they would head over to the home of a highly-recommended and trusted lesson teacher. In my circleof friends with children, we regularly exchanged information about the best lesson teachers available who could get our children ready to take the common entrance exams for admission into King's College, Queen'sCollege, or any of our other preferred schools.

We hired dedicated drivers to transport our children from one classto another across Lagos. There was the teacher in the Jibowu area of Yaba, who held all her lessons under a tree, no matter the weather. Therewas Mrs Durand in Ikoyi, one of the very best and highly sought-after.

The pace was frantic. I felt, as we all did, terribly sorry for our children, all smart by any standards, but all of whom had to endure the torture.

There were the mandatory registrations and preliminary attempts, practice runs of sorts, at the common entrance several years before they were old enough to be admitted into secondary school.

We would race to drop them off at the exam centres, waiting for them for hours on end. There was one unforgettable day outside of King's College, when we, the parents, waited to pick up our kids as it rained heavily.

I had a rude awakening when I decided to explore the almighty King's College, stepping into one of the classrooms. I was numb with shock by what I saw—a decrepit room with broken windows, and chairswith at least one broken leg.

I couldn't believe it. Was this why we were putting our children through such rigorous, demanding schedules? To spend six years of secondary school studying under such abysmal conditions? What message would we be sending to our children? To accept disorder as a normal standard of life?

I remembered how envious I'd been of my peers in university whohad been privileged to attend reputable schools like Queen's College, King's College, International School, Ibadan, Igbobi College, and Government College, Ibadan, whilst I was miserable in various boardingschools in England. What happened to these once great institutions?

How I had envied the camaraderie of those young undergraduatesat the University of Lagos, all of whom had bonded from years spent together at their formidable secondary schools.

After the jarring experience of seeing King's College in such a state, I had an 'Aha!' moment—we, my sisters and I, needed to set up ourown school.

Even the winner of the argument has a hard timesleeping.

— Takashima Gyokutoro, Japanese Poet

I wish my thirty-something-year-old self had had a book like *Jump On Board: High-Performing Not-For-Profit Boards in Fundraising* by Melissa Smith, a fantastic must-read guide on the dos and don'ts of setting up an effective board for any company wishing to endure. We would not have madethe grave error of assuming that simply because we were all sisters, andfriends, we could work well together on a board for such an ambitious project designed to succeed, grow and outlive us.

It seems ridiculous to me that amongst the five of us, we can't, till this day, even agree on who came up with the idea for the school.It's downright ludicrous that amongst us five best friends, this remains apoint of contention! This singular fact, as irrelevant as it might sound to outsiders, has caused incalculable hurt and damaged relationships.

Some have even suggested that we all five came up with the idea simultaneously at the same moment. There is no greater truism than the saying, "Success has many parents; failure is an orphan."

The facts of how we proceeded, though, are indisputable.

The first formal meeting to discuss the setting up of a co- educational secondary school was held in my house, 24B Oduduwa Street, on 18 January 1986. This was followed by a second meeting heldon 25 January 1986 at 6 Cappa Avenue, Palm Grove Estate, Ikorodu Road, the home of my sister, Mrs Gbemi Smith. I quote the minutes of that meeting verbatim:

Minutes of the meeting held on Saturday, 25 January 1986, at 6 Cappa Avenue, Ikorodu Road, to discuss the Proposed Secondary School.

Present were Mrs Smith, Mrs Fadayomi, Mrs Taiwo, and Mrs Dina.

AGENDA

Review of previous minutes, legal framework, accommodation and matters arising.

The meeting began with the review of the minutes of the previous meeting and the progress made on the various actionsto be taken.

Mrs Fadayomi gave a report on her assessment of the legal framework provided by Mrs Taiwo, which was used in setting up Grange Educational Trust, after a careful study of the file.

Based on this report, there was a general agreement that a similar framework should be used in setting up the proposed school.

The foundation members would be given some nominal shares,in lieu of their efforts in originating the concept and motivating the successful take off of the school.

In addition to the nominal shares, the foundation members would have to pay for the remaining shares when called uponto do so.

Shareholding of 20,000 ordinary shares was proposed. Foundation members would be given 5 ordinary shares each, whilst 3,000 shares would be fully paid between them.

The shareholders would be responsible for selecting the board. The debenture holders would have no say on the board. Their debenture would represent a long-term loan to the school, repayable within a stated period of time, at a nominal interestrate, in view of the non-profit nature of the project.

The other benefit for the debenture holders would be their right to place an agreed number of the children of their staff at any given time into the school, provided that the children pass the entrance examination into the school.

The members of the company were listed as Mrs Taiwo, Mrs Dina, Mrs Towry-Coker, Mrs Fadayomi and Mrs Smith.

There was a general consensus that in view of the enormous amount of work ahead, it would be necessary to enlarge the foundation membership to include other dynamic persons withsimilar goals, who could play an active role in the implementationof the project.

The need to screen thoroughly this enlarged membership was however stressed to ensure that only individuals who had a total meeting of the minds of our aspirations, as well as those with ability to play active roles, would be invited to join the company.

The following names were suggested as additional members for the company: Mrs Funke Fadayomi, Mrs Lola Akintola, Mrs Yinka Lawson, Dr Christopher Kolade, Mr Babalola, Mrs KejiOkunowo, Ambassador Adesola, Dr Bello, Alhaji Mukhtar Bello, and Miss Toyin Dabiri. Mrs Eniola Fadayomi suggestedMrs Marlies Allan, and her sister, Miss Bode Thomas.

Everyone present in the meeting was asked to discuss the conceptwith the individual they had nominated and report back to the meeting, care being taken in the selection of the individuals we were nominating.

The name of the company was widely debated. Mrs Smith had compiled a list of inspiring names as possible names for the school. Atlantic Hall/Royal Hall appeared to be the namespreferred by all.

In view of this, Abdulai Taiwo & Co would be contacted toset up a company named Atlantic Hall Limited. It was alsoagreed that in our future discussions, the registration of Atlantic Hall as a limited liability company would be assumed to havebeen completed.

Mrs Taiwo mentioned a discussion she had held with Prof C.O. Taiwo and his advice that we should obtain without delayan application form from the Ministry of Education, and study their requirements and the provisions of the laws governing the setting up of a secondary school. (Action: Mrs Smith)

Mrs Smith handed over to Mrs Taiwo the prospectus of Cranleigh School, a public school in England, with a view of helping her in the preparation of the prospectus for Atlantic Hall.

She also promised to send several other prospectuses of good public schools in the UK within the week.

UNIFORM

The question of the school uniform was discussed and it was agreed that the school uniform colour should fit the Tropics—mauve or yellow skirt and pinafore, with white shirt and a school hat.

Dr Dina was mandated to propose a logo and motto for the school by the next meeting.

IMMEDIATE PLANS

It was agreed that prior to calling the first general meeting of all the shareholders, the following action should be taken:

1) *Registration of the Company – Action: Abdulai Taiwo& Co.*
2) *Location of Accommodation – All Members*
3) *Preliminary Budget – Mrs Taiwo*
4) *Preparation of the prospectus – Mrs Taiwo*
5) *Study of the provisions of the laws governing the settingup of private secondary school – Mrs Fadayomi*

Having identified the above actions, the meeting was adjournedto a site inspection of vacant properties which had been identifiedby Mrs Taiwo as a possible site for the school. One particularsite on the GRA was found to be very suitable.

The property was inspected and everyone agreed that it had enormous potentials. Aside from having large grounds and net usable areas, the atmosphere of the neighbourhood fitted our set goals. In addition, its proximity to the country club and saddleclub was thought to be very advantageous.

Mrs Taiwo was mandated to contact Messrs' Jide Taiwo &Co., the estate agents, to find out details of the offer of lease. This was to be presented at the next meeting.

The next meeting was scheduled for the 1st of February, 1986, at 12 p.m. Venue: Dr Dina's house, this is to be the last caucus meeting prior to inviting the enlarged group to the meeting.

In this meeting, details of the budget, prospectus, modus operandi, etc.

The meeting ended at 5:00 p.m. with the renewed commitment of everyone present, to ensure the successful implementation of the project.

And so began the long tortuous journey towards the dream of establishing Atlantic Hall.

Today, Atlantic Hall sits resplendent on its permanent site in Poka Village, Epe, a co-educational, full boarding school with approximately 650 students. It has earned a considerable reputation for excellence, with alumni of some 2,000 former students holding responsible positions all over the world. In 2017, the school achieved the impressive feat of having the best overall results in the West African Educational Council (WAEC) school-leaving exam. Its alumni include Seye Ogunlewe, one of the fastest runners in Nigeria. Recently, it was adjudged during the rigorous adjudication exercise conducted on over 4,000 private secondary schools by the Lagos State Government's Ministry of Education as one of only ten outstanding schools in Lagos State.

In our wildest dreams, we could never have envisaged that our vision would reach so far.

Unknown to us in 1986 when we started on this long journey of establishing the school, there would be obstacles along the path that we couldn't have anticipated. It is to all of our credit that we remained undaunted by every obstruction, and forged ahead relentlessly, convinced that was our call to duty.

We expanded our initial group of five trustees to include five additional trustees: Miss Aboderin, Mrs Funke Fadayomi, Mrs Marlies Allan, Miss Bode Thomas, and Mrs Keji Okunowo.

Atlantic Hall was registered as a not-for-profit under the Land (Perpetual Succession) Act.

We quickly recognised that we needed the backing of some strong pillars of society to successfully execute the project, and were fortunate that exceptional leaders such as Professor C.O. Taiwo OBE, renowned educationist; Chief C.O. Ogunbanjo, a doyen of the legal profession anda leading industrialist; and Professor Oladipo Akinkugbe, a colossus in the field of medicine, accepted our invitation to be patrons.

We were almost blindsided when we were informed by Professor Taiwo that the Lagos State Government, under the regime of the then Governor, Alhaji Lateef Jakande, had compulsorily taken over all existing missionary schools, and effectively banned the establishment of private secondary schools in Lagos.

For some reason, he harboured great resentment towards private secondary schools or any institution he considered elitist, completely failing to appreciate that what he termed 'elitism' was often a reflectionof superior educational standards. In the process, he inflicted incalculable damage to some of the best privately-owned schools of the day, many established by missionaries.

Although he has been out of office since 31 December 1983, whenthe coup that brought in Major General Muhammed Buhari took place, the ban on the establishment of private secondary schools was still in place when we started our preliminary meetings on Atlantic Hall in 1986.

We refused to be daunted by what appeared to be a brutal blowto our vision; we made spirited efforts to explore the possibility of establishing the school in Ogun State instead.

Chief Moyo Aboderin, the father of two of our trustees, very kindly and generously offered us land in Ota, Ogun State. We also explored the possibility of setting up the school in Agbara Estate—also in Ogun State—where one of our members, Yinka Lawson's in-laws hadlarge holdings. In addition, our mother, Chief Mrs A.O. Shonibare, alsooffered us land in Ogudu.

It soon became clear to us, as we assessed all available options, that to get our project moving on a firm footing, we needed to change strategy. We needed to get a critical mass of like-minded parents who were experiencing the same angst as we were, to buy into our project andforce the change we desired.

With that goal in mind, we invited many of our friends and acquaintances to a stakeholders' forum held in Elephant House in 1987,to articulate our vision and invite them to join the Atlantic Hall Council, through which we hoped to move our project forward.

It was reassuring to learn that so many young parents were as frustrated as we were to be in this untenable situation, frustrated that we could not hope to provide for our children the excellent educational legacy our parents had so lovingly provided for us. We were all in agreement that that was our call to duty.

In the process of setting up the school, we discovered and were encouraged to learn, that Queen's College had been founded by a groupof women: Lady Abayomi, Lady Ademola, amongst others. The Corona School Trust Council, which established the excellent Corona Primary Schools in Ikoyi, Victoria Island, Apapa, and Gbagada, was also founded by women, members of the Corona Society. That was truly inspiring to know, and gave us tremendous courage and impetus. Our parents and grandparents had changed the educational landscape in Nigeria by their pioneering efforts, leaving us a legacy to replicate, if we dared.

The membership of the council grew, and through the obligatory membership fee, earned us some much-needed additional income to support the running of our organisation. We established key committees through which the integral work of setting up the school was carried out—the Finance Committee, Educational Committee, and the Landand Building Committee.

We owe a debt of gratitude to the members who served on these committees and worked tirelessly for the realisation of our dream. Through their chairing the various committees at different times, they were also nominated members of the board.

They include:

- Mr M. Iyayi
- Mr N. Onamuti
- Mr T. Munis
- Mrs Ojutalayo

- Dr Mrs N. Onyekwe
- Mr A. Shonibare
- Dr Mrs B. Tilley Gyado
- Ms Toyin Dabiri
- Mr Jimi Agbaje
- Mrs F Sowole
- Mrs F.N. de Souza
- Mr Dapo Shogbola
- Ms Dupe Irele
- Ms A.K. David
- Dr S. Sobanjo
- Mr T. Cardoso
- Ms I.T. David
- Mrs S. Oyemade
- Mrs I. Akerele
- Mr L.A. Nedd
- Dr Mrs M. Onuzo
- Mr D.A. Omole
- Mrs Sylvia Bello

We simply couldn't have achieved what we did without their commitment and relentless efforts.

There were many moments of frustration along the way; sometimes, itfelt as if we were going round in circles!

One positive development for our project was the appointmentof Captain Michael Akhigbe as the new governor of Lagos State. He revised the previous law imposed by the Jakande regime banning the establishment of private secondary schools in the state. We could, at last, take a giant leap forward with our school project.

We pulled our energies together towards raising the needed capitalfor the project. A committee was set up to plan a fundraising event which would, in effect, be our first public outing. We owe enormous gratitude to my great friend, Nikue Akpe, who had suggested we feature a thirteen-year-old child prodigy, Sodi Braide, at the event.

He had completed his high school at an astronomic speed bythe age of twelve, completing the six years in three years. Beyond his academic genius, he was also a talented concert pianist who had recently won the Junior Nobel Prize in Music. I was not aware that such an award even existed. At the event, which had involved meticulous planning, Sodi's genius performance was the *pièce de résistance*.

Atlantic Hall Educational Trust Council's Inaugural Dinner took place on 27 February 1986, at the Eko Holiday Inn. Our guests included top business and government leaders, ministers, diplomats. The event was held under the distinguished chairmanship of Chief Christopher Ogunbanjo.

We introduced our vision for Atlantic Hall, an institution that would be a centre of excellence and integrity, where we would nurture, primarily, Nigerian children, with a focus on supporting a comprehensive development of each child. Our students would be educated to excel, not just in Nigeria, their home country, but in any part of our ever-changing world.

Everyone in attendance identified strongly with our mission. Evidently, having Sodi perform at the event had the desired effect. His piano performance was indeed flawless; some guests who attended believed our aim in setting up Atlantic Hall was to produce many Sodi Braides!

The money raised at this event, roughly ₦125,000—which isnot a lot of money today with the naira being severely devalued—was consequential in 1988. It was certainly enough to enable us to, at last, take a major step in moving our project forward.

A post-event meeting was held, during which I was formally nominated Founding Chairman. The meeting also included the appointment of our patrons, our four pillars: Professor C.O. Taiwo OBE, Chief Christopher Ogunbanjo, Dr Christopher Kolade, and Professor Ladipo Akinkugbe. In addition, we took the unanimous decision to appoint Chief Dele Fajemirokun, who had been the most generous donor at the inaugural dinner, as patron, no matter that he was much younger than our other patrons.

We also decided we needed to hire a secretary to manage our secretariat. It had been my lot to write most of the minutes up to this point.It was agreed that Mr Biodun Davis would be the secretary, following a rigorous exercise to determine the best candidate, by Mr Onamuti. He operated out of a small office within my office, and from day one, I was extremely impressed with his ability to write excellent minutes.

Despite our sometimes disorderly and unruly meetings, he had an impressive ability to cut all the inessential and irrelevant aspects, and record, in a remarkable way, the simple, vital facts and decisions reached, clearly and succinctly, written with impeccable grammar.

Davis remains with us to this day, as the Executive Secretaryof Atlantic Hall Trust Council. He has served loyally under ten (10) Chairmen of the board. He is extraordinarily tactful and sanguine.

We decided at that meeting, to commence our project by securinga temporary site, which could serve the needs of the school. The idea of building a permanent site on any of the various parcels of land, which had been generously offered, was simply unrealistic. How on earth couldwe possibly fund such an enormous venture? All the more out of our reach as banks at the time simply would not lend money for executing aschool project. They could not conceive the viability of such a project. The typical short-sightedness of banking institutions!

The irony is today, every single major bank considers school projects as cash cows, and aggressively pursue their accounts.

We asked a few agents to help us search for a potential temporarysite. It had become evident by now, that it was no longer to be a small secondary school with a maximum student population of 150, as we had originally envisaged. It would be a much larger enterprise, with a student population of 100 per annum in five streams. That was indeed a tall order.

We were shown a number of properties, most of them in horrendous states of disrepair. We had very specific requirements—a site that had the capacity for accommodation, with dozens of rooms, administrative blocks, and dining hall space.

It was proving to be near impossible to find such a space. We founda large house on Airport Road that had once belonged to the Mumunis. Ithad several rooms, about six or seven. The late Alhaji Mumuni had been polygamous, which explained why he had built such a sprawling property, but it had long been abandoned, taken over by Fulani nomads who had created their colony on the property.

The state of the property was abysmal, seriously dilapidated. Coupled with that was there was barely any ground left. The house more or less occupied the entire space. Plus, we were asked to pay rent three years in advance, a common practice in Nigeria at the time, until very recently when the property market crashed.

It was a frustrating experience, and we were fast growing despondent.

But then, I realised the solution was right under our noses—our Maryland Hotel. Set on three and a half acres of land, on the serene Shonibare Estate, with its fifty double bedrooms, a swimming pool in the quadrangle of the main building, and other stand-alone buildings, perhaps that could be our temporary site. The Beachcomber, which had been the location of the funky discotheque of the 70s; La Parisienne, a hundred-seater restaurant; the separate eight-unit single bedrooms; an administrative block…

The more we looked at it, the more it became clear it could be theideal solution we were looking for. It was truly another 'Aha!' moment. A sixty-bed hotel perfectly converted into a school.

Once other members had agreed on this, all we needed to do was convince my mother to let us take up the lease of the property, without paying in advance; instead, 'payable when able'. It would mean halting the redevelopment plan for the Maryland Hotel and permitting us to proceed with the fundamental changes needed to convert the hotelto a school. In effect, this would render a conversion back to a hotel permanently unviable.

My mother agreed with the plan and gave her blessings, especiallyas we'd pointed out we were, in part, doing it for her grandchildren. Wealso assured her we would not be there for more than five years. Atlantic

Hall ended up staying in the temporary site at Maryland for fifteen (15)years!

A fair bit of work still had to be done. Money had to be raised, which we accomplished with interest-free loans from some of us, to execute the significant work and expenditure required in the conversionconstruction; acquisition of equipment and kitting out various science labs, classrooms, a school hall, dining rooms, and other essentials we were quickly learning were critical to establishing a bona fide co-educational secondary school.

We owe a huge debt of gratitude to all those who worked tirelessly and gave so much in cash and kind to enable the launch of the school.

As of the year 2020, I am delighted to share that Atlantic Hall is now thirty years old. It is a full boarding school with over 600 students, a beautiful, purpose-built permanent site in the serene location of Poka Village, Epe. It continues to garner national and international accolades including being one of only four schools deemed, by the Lagos State Quality Control Department of the Ministry of Education, to be outstanding, based on our showing in the West African Examination Council (WAEC) exams, with the best results in Nigeria for the years 2018, 2019 and 2020. We also had the best overall IGCSE (International General Certificate of Secondary Education) results in the years 2019 and 2020.

We have formed international partnerships with Carleton University of Ottawa, Canada, offering multiple opportunities, includinga two-year preliminary programme, leading to the direct entry of our students to the prestigious Carleton University.

Quoted from the 2019 Anniversary Speech:

> *Carleton University, Ottawa, Canada, and Atlantic Hall School, Epe, Lagos, Nigeria, are forging a unique partnership, which promises to take the buoyant educational ties between Nigeria and Canada to the next level. Discussions commencedat the Nigeria Canada Investment Summit in Abuja in2019, under the watchful eyes and commitment of His Excellency, Ambassador Adeyinka Asekun, the Nigerian High Commissioner to Canada, who saw the enormous potential that existed in consolidating the remarkable educational links between Nigeria and Canada. This laudable initiative was directed by the ingenious Professor Tony Bailetti, the Director of Carleton University's Technology Innovation Management Program, guided by the dynamic, and quietly*

resourceful Professor Dana Brown, Dean of the Sprott School of Business at Carleton University, and her team, and coordinated by my humble self, Chief Mrs Taiwo Taiwo, Chairman, Board of Trustees of Atlantic Hall. I was ably assisted by our very diligent and focused team at Atlantic Hall consisting of Andrew Jedras and Dr Tunji Abimbola among others.

We are profoundly excited that this unique partnership, which portends limitless opportunities for both our institutions, is coming in a year we are celebrating our 30th anniversary, and have made a commitment to take Atlantic Hall from Great to Greatest.

"Congratulations for this milestone! I am delighted to hear the news and wish to commend you both for your leadership.

On behalf of the many people, who will benefit from your leadership for many years to come, THANK YOU!"

"This is one of those wonderful moments in life when I feel great pride of being a Carleton University faculty member and so fortunate to have had the opportunity to meet Ms Taiwo Taiwo, both in Abuja and in Lagos last November."

"I remember arriving in Abuja last November (with no bags!) with a long 'to do' list. I asked His Excellency, Adeyinka Asekun, who the right person was to speak about one of the most important topics in my 'to do' list. Before I could finish the question, His Excellency looked at me, and said, "Talk to my sister, Taiwo Taiwo." He grabbed my hand and walked me over to Ms Taiwo Taiwo, and introduced us. The rest is a wonderful story of Nigeria-Canada leadership and commitment."

"Finally, I would like to say THANK YOU! To my colleague Dr Stoyan Tanev who led this initiative at the School. He is a wonderful colleague to work with and since our first meeting where the program was shaped, he has worked non-stop to ensure that the program will be a successful one."

"Once again, Dr Dana Brown and Mrs Taiwo Taiwo, we offer a huge round of noisy applause to celebrate this milestone (Nigerian + Latin American loud applause, not soft Canadianpolite clap clap)." Professor, Tony Bailetti.

"This is such heart-warming news and clearly a milestone during our time in Canada to date," said His Excellency Adeyinka O. Asekun, Nigerian High Commissioner to Canada.

"I would like to acknowledge and appreciate all the hard work and tenacity on the part of various individuals that have made this possible. To Dean Dana Brown and her team at Carletonand Chief Taiwo Taiwo and her team at Atlantic Hall, I say kudos and congratulations! I believe the success of this well thought out collaboration will inspire and encourage many more such initiatives," His Excellency, Adeyinka O. Asekun.

With our other partner, the Worldreader organisation, we offer digital books from over four hundred publishers. We are in advanced discussions with the United World Colleges to explore the possibility ofbeing their first partner school in West Africa.

Undoubtedly, the school is an enormous success, but our success did come at a price in the form of irreparably broken relationships. Evennow, in our middle ages, some friendships have deteriorated to the pointof no return, with former friends seemingly hell-bent on hurting each other.

It was a life lesson I am so happy I had learnt years ago when I read Judith Viorst's perceptive book, *Necessary Losses*. I recommend it to everyone, it will most certainly enrich and absorb anyone who admits to being human.

Judith Viorst, a brilliant clinical psychologist, takes us through a chilling but compelling narrative of the fact that life, at the end of the day, from the moment we are ejected from the cocoon of our mother's womb to face the harsh glare of light, is a series of necessary losses. Losses from which on each occasion, we are given the opportunity to learn and grow.

A DREAM GONE UP IN SMOKE?

Three years after settling down in Elephant House, it was clear we had to address some critical financial issues about the construction of the building.

The insurance companies, who had ALL committed to taking outthe bridge financiers at the end of the construction, and had signed onto the Debenture Trust Deed, did not keep to their end of the bargain. It didn't matter that we had paid each one of them a 1% commitment fee at the commencement of the project.

Six months before the expected handover date of the building,we informed them of the imminent completion of the project, and gave them notice of their obligation to redeem their commitment to takeout the bridge financiers in the various stipulated ratios and as per the Debenture Trust Deed to the consortium. However, on completion, not one of them fulfilled their obligations!

Apparently, they had not put much thought into what they were committing to when they attended the grand completion board meeting years back. From all indications, they were more interested in pocketing the commitment fee we paid to each of them, perhaps thinking that it was a freebie of sorts that required nothing from them. Unbelievable!

To complicate matters further, UBA Plc., the lead bank in our consortium of bridge financiers, who had taken up a lease on the 8th to 12th floors, had pulled a fast one on us. It strictly involved the antics of the bank's property department.

When it came to measuring the net lettable floor area of eachof our floors, against all professional and best practices, they deducted, in their calculations, every pillar skirting space, every installed air-conditioning space, lobby space, and toilet areas from the net lettable space. This meant they paid us less than the market rate for these floors. From a lettable area of 6,000 square feet per floor, they reduced our net lettable area per floor to 5,200 squares.

Their hard-bargaining MD, Alhaji Mutallab, wouldn't let up. However, despite this incident, to this day I still consider him a dear friend.

It was a double whammy, quite brutal on our rental income, exacerbating cash flow problems we were experiencing at the end ofa massive speculative development which had taken every bit of our internally generated resources, in addition to the bank loans and rents in advance, to complete.

I was being hounded by contractors for retention. The irony was people around me, including members of my family, thought I was some privileged heiress with not a care in the world. If they only knew.

At a certain point, I took to not answering my phone, terrified of being cornered by another one of our creditors. The last thing I wanted to hear was the accusatory tone in their voices.

But I plodded on, pressing hard to get the funds from the insurance companies. Surely, with signed documents in place, they were obliged to pay those funds?

Everything came to a head one fine day when I received a call from my very dear friend, Nikue Akpe, who happened to be an executivedirector at UBA Plc., and at that time, Chairman of UBA Trustees.

"Taiwo, we need to talk," he said.

He came over to my office.

"What's going on with Elephant House?" he asked. "Why are UBA Trustees broaching the subject of a receiver-manager to take over your company?"

I explained everything to him, wondering why I hadn't done so sooner, him being a trusted friend. I was completely honest and vulnerable with him, sharing my frustrations and anxieties of the past two years.

He listened intently and made some very reassuring suggestions. He would make sure that the idea of receiver-manager would be off the table in any meeting at UBA Trustees, as long as he was Chairman. Theywould also do their bit to compel the insurance companies to pay off their commitment, giving us time to straighten things out.

I consulted my mother, the ever calm, insightful, and pragmatic businesswoman that she was.

"What is the problem, my husband?" she asked, my concerns and anxieties impossible to hide from a mother who knew me so well.

I told her the whole story. She was, of course, aware of some of my frustrations, including the antics of the UBA property department, as I consulted with her daily, either stopping by her house on my way to work or returning there in the evening on my way back.

I recall years later, a close friend of mine on hearing this, screeched, "You mean you see your mummy every day? Taiwo, really!"

Well, roll your eyes all you want. I knew the enormity of the loadshe had handed over to me. I knew jolly well that she trusted me to makeall the right decisions, but I also knew her invaluable, insightful analysesof issues were always on point.

"*Ku ise*, my husband." *Well done, my husband.* She said this to me almost daily. What would I have done without her love and support?

"So, what is our total exposure to all our creditors? What do you think we need to do?" she asked.

Instantly, I felt comforted by her show of concern and explained to her that if the insurance companies could pay up their commitmentof close to ₦4.5 million, we would be in a position to liquidate our obligations to our bridge financiers, and then deal with the long-term creditors over the next five years.

She asked calmly, "What do we need to do to clear off all our debts, so that we owe nobody?"

I explained that if we could convince UBA to re-measure their floors accurately, get them to lease the two remaining floors in ElephantHouse, and pay us five years in advance, we would be home and dry, andthen some.

"Well then. That is exactly what we must do!" she said.

I was suddenly invigorated. That's it. A two-pronged strategy to solve the problem in one scoop.

I started by putting pen to paper and writing an appeal letter for my life. Truly, I felt my life depended on it.

I couched it along with a deep and heartfelt appeal to the Chairmanof UBA, Chief Mrs Kuforiji Olubi, renowned for being fearless and formidable. I used all the guiles in my arsenal—pathos, nationalism, patriotism, feminism—any and every tool I could employ:

> *We were an indigenous company that had pioneered residential real estate in Nigeria. We are now pioneering the commercial real estate market, with the construction of the iconic Elephant House.*
>
> *We had achieved, against all odds, the construction of the 18-storey office block, completed in record time and to budget.*
>
> *We had utilised all our internally-generated resources from our residential estate to pay interests and complete the project.*
>
> *UBA, our lead bank, had failed to support our project to ensure that we were in a position to liquidate our bridge loans to them.*
>
> *They had incorrectly measured the five floors leased from us, paying us below market rate. They owed hardworking, pioneering Nigerian*

businesses, like ours, a duty to ensure their survival. They should not be the ones impeding our ability to fulfill our obligations to them.

It would be a shame for the failure of this landmark project to be due to their inability to pay the right rent, and measure our floors in an equitable manner...

Finally, I made my pitch:

We insist that they re-measure the floors, take up the three remaining vacant office space, and finally pay us five years in advance on the five floors whose leases were due for renewal, with a further three years in advance for the three new floors they would take.

I finished the letter, signing off on it, satisfied that I had written a compelling letter that should sell our case.

A personal copy of the letter to Chief Mrs Kuforiji Olubi was delivered, personally, by my mother. I knew, jolly well, not to tread where my elders' steps were required.

That was it; the deal was sealed. My instincts had been proven correct. There were still paths where it was infinitely easier for Mummyto tread. A meeting of the consortium of lenders to the Elephant House trust deed was scheduled.

In addition to our bridge financiers, First Bank of Nigeria, United Bank for Africa, International Bank for West Africa, and Niger Insurance, were also on the unwieldy list of debenture lenders, headed by NICON Insurance.

Before the meeting, my husband and I paid a visit to ChiefAdeyemi who was, at the time, the Chief Legal Adviser of NICON. He fully briefed him on the status of the project. I explained to him thatthe project had been extremely successful but had suffered a hitch on completion because not one of the insurance companies—including his company, NICON, being the leader of the insurance companies who hadcommitted to taking out the bridge financiers at the end of the project and collected a commitment fee from us to boot—had done so in the end.

Chief Adeyemi, to whom I remain eternally grateful, assured us he would personally attend the meeting.

He was a doyen of sorts amongst the heads of the insurance companies. They all had tremendous respect for him which gave us an enormous amount of confidence with his presence at the meeting. Both the bridge and long-term financiers concluded that the project had been efficiently executed and creatively funded.

I arrived at the meeting with Mum. It was held in the rather intimidating boardroom of UBA, packed with bankers, lawyers, and other professionals. I confidently made my introductory remarks, all mynerves of the last month had disappeared. I thanked all of them for the confidence they had placed in us by funding our project.

There was one particularly nasty employee of NICON, mid-management, who liked to flex his muscles, and had been particularly unpleasant to our team over the past few months. He'd, at some point, even stated that lending money to women always posed a problem, as they were prone to use the money to go off and buy jewellery. Can you imagine?

Throughout the meeting, he tried to get a word in, but his boss, Chief Adeyemi, reminded him that he represented the institution at the meeting.

My mother, in a stern voice, reminded him of his foolish, archaic beliefs about lending money to women. She gave it to him without missing a beat.

But the final *coup de grâce*, known only to my mother and myself, was left to the very end of the meeting.

"How much, by the way, is the outstanding sum we owe on the project? Both bridge and debenture?" I asked.

By this point in the meeting, we had concluded on the extension of the UBA lease on Elephant House, and had been paid the advance.

In quite the dramatic fashion, I whipped out a cheque from my purse, and said, "With this, I believe, we have fully liquidated all our commitments to each and every one of you."

Mic. Drop.

"It was nice doing business with you."

The silence in the room was palpable. My mother later told me she had never been more proud of me than at that very moment. They all rushed to shake our hands excitedly, stating how much it had been a pleasure doing business with us.

Afterwards, I was informed we had been the first institution in the history of the capital market to complete such a payment as and when due. I was relieved and elated to see the end of that project.

A FAMILY IN TURMOIL

Although we'd liquidated our debts on Elephant House, we'd done so from rent payments collected five years in advance—which, in effect, meant we were not expecting rental revenues from most of the floors in Elephant House for several years to come. We, thus, had to operate with discipline and keep a tight leash on our cash flow.

Unknown to me, another family plot against me was brewing, inevitably by the same protagonists, who had always been able to spin fantastic yarns.

That was the era when Nigeria witnessed the first pyramid and Ponzi schemes, traps that many, unbelievably, fell for, some of whom were intelligent, savvy, and urbane.

My brother, Alaba, who had resigned or retired from the company some years earlier, bored, as he said, of being a glorified rent collector, decided to explore other business avenues for generating income.

There were many dubious financial institutions at the time, operating unregulated, all over Nigeria. Even the Central Bank did nothing to curb those suspicious business practices.

You could deposit any amount in multiple of millions, and be paid rates of 25%, 30%, 40%, or higher, on your deposit per annum, even though the deposit could be placed for a period of one month or more. It was an obvious red flag. Surely, any rational mind would or should have known it could not be legitimate; there was no possible way a business like that was viable.

Nevertheless, these schemes took off like the Concorde, perhaps more like a satellite launched to the moon, and flourished, with zero interference from financial regulating authorities.

People queued to deposit their life savings, their pensions; some even sold their homes and placed the proceeds of the sale into one of these ludicrous schemes. The herd mentality was in full effect.

> Men, it has been well said, think in herds; it willbe seen that they go mad in herds, while they onlyrecover their senses slowly, and one by one.
>
> — Charles Mackay, *Extraordinary Popular Delusionsand the Madness of Crowds*

My brother, Alaba, always fancied himself a wheeler-dealer, never known for any real original thought, but rather prone to pick out, and participate in, the newest scheme in town, certain that it would be the next best thing. As he so often did, he would try to sell the scheme-of- the-moment to others, sometimes passing it off as his own brilliant idea.

So began Alaba's determination to pull our family business into that madness.

He had written, as usual, an in-depth proposal, never one for brevity. The idea was that we sell every single property on our ShonibareEstate, releasing huge capital for the company. The way he articulated it, we would be released from the burden of those assets which, from his conclusions, were earning us peanuts in rental income, all completely debt free with a 100% occupancy rate. He thought we should place all the funds in the 'money market', as those dubious schemes were called,and *voila*, we would be receiving multi-millions every month for doing absolutely nothing!

My mother was speechless, utterly flabbergasted.

She thought it a crazy idea, but not everyone saw it that way, unfortunately. Some family members were intrigued, loved the idea even.

Instant cash on hand to live the dream of the idle rich!

I remember Alaba coming to me and trying so earnestly to sell this warped idea to me.

Ever eager to be as gentle with him as I could, I tried a compromise.

"Why don't we start by selling one duplex, and placing the revenue from the sale into the scheme? Let's see how that would work?" I asked.

He was terribly disappointed.

"Oh no. That would not do it." He was adamant that we shouldgo all in, and reap the zillions we stood to gain.

My mother, on the other hand, ever the shrewd businesswoman she was, put her foot down hard, with an emphatic "No!" She was havingnone of it.

That experience so alarmed and shocked her that it, undoubtedly, spurred her to contemplate estate planning. She consulted some of the smartest lawyers, accountants, and other consultants around, before making a decision.

She summoned us all to her office at the Maryland Villa, from where she operated and proceeded to lay out her plans.

She was tired of the constant bickering amongst her children, andto put an end to it, she had decided to divide the bulk of her estate equally amongst her children. She gave each one of us our allotted properties, and was scrupulous in the manner in which she ensured each of us got the same quantum.

To those who wished to follow Alaba in his foolhardy ventureof participating in the Ponzi scheme, she gave a block of six flats and two townhouses, plus three townhouses for them to sell and put in their 'money market' scheme.

Four of them chose this path, although to be fair, it is not clear to me if my elder sister, Ronke, had given her consent to be a part of, for lack of a better phrase, 'the gang of four'.

Ronke had been missing in action for some years, paralysed by marital problems she simply could not or would not share with any one of us, including our mother, with whom she had once been so close.

Instead, she dove deep into religion, which seemed to have completely taken over her life. To me, it felt like she'd joined a cult—there was really no other way to describe this 'religious' institution to which she'd devoted her life. Tragically, she'd become entrapped in this 'cult' tothe exclusion of family and friends, including her two lovely daughters.

We were all heartbroken; my mother was simply devastated. Theremust be a special place in hell reserved for leaders of such cults—cruel manipulators who prey on the vulnerable, all in the name of religion.

Rather melodramatically, Mummy called us all to her study, gaveus all the relevant legal documents—deed of assignment in each of our names to the various properties assigned to us. She prayed for us all, wished us all the best in our future endeavours, and informed us shehad given us 'our inheritance', our birthright, as my brother would oftendescribe it.

She left the complex work of how a company could give away the bulk of its assets to shareholders who owned only 10% shares in the company to be worked out by her corporate lawyers, Abdulai Taiwo & Co., whom she always consulted when working out the legal aspects of complicated corporate issues; and Anderson Consultant to sort out the restructuring of the company with its new ownership structure.

From that moment on, in 1993, each of us was the landlord of the various properties allocated to us, collecting rent on them.

It was not much of a surprise to learn that the big money market scheme, which had been entered into by the gang of four, failed woefully. As I'd expected, the Ponzi scheme eventually collapsed on the weight of collecting enormous deposits from one set of investors and paying them the eye-popping interests from subsequent depositors.

Like a pack of cards, it fell, shattering the lives of millions; ruining the lives of many upper- and middle-class families in Nigeria.

'Kincadine', a name I'd registered some years earlier for the company, as a vehicle for future prospective business ventures, was the name used by the gang of four to transact their genius money market scheme.

Its failure was as dramatic as anyone could have expected, but onepart did not fail totally. They had been convinced by 'Mr Wheeler Dealer' to reinvest part of the land they sold and have him build townhouses on them, before putting what remained back into the money market.

At the final account and post mortem of Kincadine, there was no money left. Alaba had to complete the houses he had started to buildto sell; I recollect that he had to lend the company his own money to complete the townhouses, and naturally, he had to recoup his money once those townhouses were sold. What a messy saga.

The whole episode epitomises for me, Charles Mackay's wise words about the herd mentality and the madness of crowds.

At least, they still had the assets assigned to them, which were still quite considerable—a block of six-bedroom flats and two townhouses.

Mummy's strategy seemed to have worked, at least for the time being. Everyone had assets from which they were collecting rental income to manage and deal with as they pleased.

Did this guarantee peace and harmony within the family? If it did,it certainly was not for long. A family that had thrived on melodrama forso long would, inevitably, find it impossible to change its pattern.

As the saying goes, *All that glitters is not gold.* So very true in the case of my family. Within five to ten years, some had doubled their inheritance, most had managed to keep it as safe investments, one sister had sold it all, plus more.

Mummy's decision to make the gutsy, truly unprecedented changein her company, seemed to have worked, for the most part. Having divided her estate equally amongst her children, consulting with the smartest management consultants and lawyers around, she proceeded torestructure her company. A complete overhaul.

She took the unprecedented decision to transfer 100% of the shares of her company to UBA Capital for a period of fifty years. No doubt about it, she wanted her children as far away from what was left of her company as possible.

Enough with the perennial fights and rivalry. I know it must have really broken her heart.

I recall her once saying, "Is it a curse to have money?

How did it come to this? My loving, close family, my beloved children, all at each other's throats."

She set up another company, Lexham Investments, which owned Shonny Investments and Properties Co. one hundred percent, which was in turn owned by UBA Capital. There were, however, some criticalcaveats in this particular structure.

The Chairman of the company, which she was during her lifetime,held exclusive decision-making powers in key areas of the business. Following Mummy's farsighted and brilliant decision to divide her estate equally amongst her children, there was a palpable, collective sigh of relief.

The constant bickering, petty jealousies, relentless plots, all stopped, like the calmness of the earth after a vicious destructive tornado. There was peace in the family, and we were able to retrieve the loving sisterlyand brotherly love we had always shared with each other.

In a large family such as ours, with eight children, there was boundto be some who were closer than others. The twins, Kehinde and myself,had an extra special bond, always had. I was extremely protective of her,and I believe she was of me. I would have taken a bullet for her.

When you are joyous, look deep in your heart andyou
will find it is only that which has given you sorrowthat is
giving you joy.

— From *On Joy and Sorrow* by Khalil Gibran

And so it was that for the next few years, the company operated inan extremely corporate manner.

My mother, years ahead of her generation, had decided to invite professional external directors to the much-reduced board, on which she was herself the Chairman; I, Managing Director (MD); my brother, Gbeyin, an Executive Director (ED).

She invited two very distinguished professionals into the fold, whom she had tremendous respect for.

Chief Gilbert Olukoya, the CEO of Pfizer Ltd., who also happenedto be her younger brother—the best way to describe their convoluted family relationship—and the revered Professor Mabogunje, a renowned geographer and banker who was Chairman of First Interstate Bank, and later, Unity Bank, a much sought-after board member in Nigerian and multinational companies.

Our meetings were extremely professional and disciplined. I relished them. We could get on with the job in the most professional manner possible, and dared to contemplate diversification and trading.

RECLAIMING DOWNTOWN LAGOS

How on earth did this insidious phenomenon plant its roots on Lagos Island, and how did we let it fester and grow until it became the oak tree it had now grown to be? A veritable well-oiled mafia machine that threatened the existence of all law-abiding citizens and institutions of Lagos Island. The proud Central Business District of Nigeria, nay, of the West African Coast of Traders, controlled by marauding miscreants? When did it begin?

'Downtown Lagos, Down the Drain' had become the slogan. Residents and investors of Lagos Island watched in horror as the Business Centre District of Lagos State and Commercial Centre of Nigeria deteriorated over the years.

Alarmed at the devaluation and depreciation of the billions of naira invested on the Island by government and private investors, and unwilling to look on helplessly while the exodus continued, a group of property owners led by me, Managing Director of Shonny Investments and Properties Co. Ltd., owners of Elephant House, 214 Broad Street, decided to take the bull by the horns, and stem the downward spiral.

An existing group, Association of Building Owners of Lagos Island (ABOLI), which had been formed and registered a couple of yearsearlier, was merged with a new initiative to form Lagos Millenium Groupon the Environment (LIMGE).

How, why had I thrown myself wholeheartedly to what was clearly going to be an extremely difficult situation to solve, with the unique mixture of a complex melee of characters thrown in? Local politicians, an entrenched mafia who served their masters, the politicians, well, and who, as I was to learn, were tactically emboldened by those masters, essential for their grassroot support in times of politics.

Undoubtedly, the most difficult task I ever embarked on in my gutsy life was my determination to arrest the takeover of Lagos Island by gangsters, arrest its deterioration, and change the trajectory of the city that seemed fated to be discarded in the dustbin of history.

Elephant House was my baby, the baby I had worked so very hardto create, and succeeded against all odds, I was not going to allow it become a 'white elephant,' as one of my siblings said with relish duringthose difficult times.

I can honestly say I did not notice the creeping up of those street urchins who would knock your car window, with you safely ensconced inside, absorbed in reading notes to your next meeting or catching up with the newspapers.

They gradually became more aggressive and audacious, banging on the doors of your cars, shamelessly demanding money, as if they hadjust won a war and were all geared to take their loot.

How could I have ignored them for so long?

Indeed, how did so many of us ignore them, cocooned in our air-conditioned cars, and for all the world, oblivious to our surroundings?

My epiphany, my 'enough is enough' moment, came one fine dayas I took the normal back route we took to my office, a five minutes detour to the centre of Lagos Island.

Was I having double vision?

Was that not a rubbish dump on Savage Lane, one of the historical lanes of Lagos Island, minutes from Elephant House?

The next week, I watched in horror as that rubbish dump had grown to become a huge mountain of waste of all sorts.

The horror of horrors, within two weeks, we simply could not pass Savage Lane to get to Elephant House!

Alas, that was just the beginning.

A week later, I noticed some pig farmers had discovered the dumpand found it ideal as the perfect 'grazing' ground for their piglets. How right they were! Within weeks, the pigs had become so fattened, they would have made a gastronomic feast on the table of the notoriously greedy Henry VIII.

I counted up to forty such pigs.

We had not reached the zenith of our fall; cow rearers soon joined,and we had cows and pigs feeding on the filthy dump on Savage Lane, inthe Central Business District of Lagos Island.

That was it for me.

I could visualise a visit to my office in the penthouse of Elephant House by foreign guests and business partners who had met me anywhere and everywhere in the world and had always remarked at my meticulous, urbane dressing and general composure.

Ha ha, I thought. *What a fake. She actually lives in a pigsty.*

I was not going to let that happen. Off I went, unstoppable, single-mindedly determined to halt the disgraceful degradation of the centre of the historical treasure of Lagos, the Central Business District of Nigeria, the heartbeat of Africa, and so began my tenacious fifteen-year journey to change the story of Lagos Island.

Using the members list of ABOLI, I simply took the bull by the horns. ABOLI was a relatively small group consisting of owners of high-rise buildings of Lagos Island.

It was the initiative of Mr Oniyangi, the then MD of NOLCHEM,who had recently completed, like us, their first-class eighteen-storey office block on Marina.

There were, if my recollection serves me well, not more than twelve high-rise modern office blocks on Lagos Island when they completed their lovely new building, almost the same time we completed the construction of Elephant House. The two buildings had been constructed by Bouygues,so we had a natural affinity to each other.

Sadly ABOLI, with all its very noble aims—cooperation on the security of all high-rises in the neighbourhood, cooperation in fighting fires in any of our properties, all undoubtedly noble ideas and a great initiative—just as it was about to take off, another one of those endless disruptive military coup d'états occurred, and inevitably all heads and Managing Directors of organisations in which the government had a majority stake, retired with immediate effect.

I participated actively in ABOLI, and was made secretary tothe group. We managed to register the group as a not-for-profit with a constitution and all.

No doubt about it, the consistent military coups that seized and changed powers in Nigeria for at least twenty years can be blamed for a whole lot of the problems Nigeria encountered for years, dare I say, till date?

The removal of Mr Oniyangi and the appointment of a new MD in NOLCHEM, inevitably, changed the focus of the new management, and alas, that was in effect the end of ABOLI, with all its enormous potential.

I truly believe that when you have a passion in your heart for a change, you absolutely must not waste a day.

Impossible for me to say exactly when the advent of the emergence of Area Boys, the totally ridiculous and rather romantic name usedto describe a decidedly unromantic, roguish group of young thugs, pickpockets, with some dangerous armed robbers thrown in the mix, began insidiously to creep into Lagos Island, the Central Business District of Nigeria.

The background, as is often the case, was political. It began duringthe tenure of Ademola Adeniji-Adele, the then Chairman of Lagos Island Local Government, who conjured the whole thing up, that the original indigenes had been completely marginalised by business leaders,market leaders—in effect, those who had made enormous investments inLagos Island—bringing with their investments, tremendous prosperity, and opportunities for those who resided in the area.

He came up with this ludicrous idea that the descendants of the original landowners, the 'Area boys', had been totally marginalised and had a right to demand ransom money from anyone coming in and out of the Island.

Crazy and totally nonsensical, it had nevertheless served him well politically when he was vying to be the chairman of the local government.

The truth in fact was very different, these were no displaced indigenes of the area, but thugs, gangsters, who very often did noteven come from the area. Many of them came from different tribes all over Nigeria, Ibos, Hausas, and any other place they could amass from anywhere in Nigeria.

As often happens, they helped him win his election by intimidating every one during the elections, and after elections began their reign of terror on law abiding citizens of the neighbourhood.

So insidious was their rise that I had no idea when it started.

I would sometimes ponder, without giving it much of a thought, engrossed as I inevitably was in my car, reading the newspaper, or going through my papers for the next meeting, Who on earth were these young thugs, banging the window of my car demanding that I give them money? What an affront. I would think!

These were not anything like the beggars which we were accustomed to seeing everywhere, especially in traffic, looking very meek and begging earnestly, praying in the name of Jesus, Allah, or both, for money. But never ever menacing, at least not overtly so

This bunch were young men, and some not so young, with blood-red eyes, aggressively banging one's windows, demanding for your money, because they were 'Area boys', boys of the neighbourhood, that had belonged to their forefathers. I assume they concluded we needed topay a toll gate pass to each one of them.

It was laughable if it wasn't that they actually meant it.

Gradually, the phenomenon of Area boys had consumed Lagos Island; that with the existing mafia of the transport union wreaked havoc on the road with the contrived traffic they engineered by packing yellow Kombi buses, the main means of transport for workers on the Island, on the major exit roads, refusing to use the bus stops, causing mayhem on the road.

Lagos Island, already suffering environmental degradation as a result of years of neglect from successive governments, simply buckled with the additional menace of area boys and Downtown Lagos, indeed went down the drain.

Downtown Lagos, the Central Business District had been transformed into a mafia gangland, with a mountain of a refuse dump, with big fat wild pigs, goats, and cows, grazing merrily next to the headquarters of property housing the most sophisticated banks, financial institutions, and oil companies.

This was my 'aha!' moment, enough is enough, I had to involve myself in my community and resolve this disgraceful, embarrassing, horrifying mess. Not a day would be wasted.

I wouldn't wait a minute longer, again my unstoppable focussed determination had been reignited. This was a job that had to be done.

I wrote a dramatic letter to all the old members of ABOLI, luckily being the secretary, I still had all their details.

> DOWNTOWN LAGOS, DOWN THE DRAIN,
>
> AND WITH IT ALL OUR ASSETS
>
> *IF YOU SHARE my conviction on the above and are unwillingto let the billions of naira we have all invested on this CBD go to waste, join me at a meeting on 8 January 1999, which I shall be pleased to host you at our boardroom on the 18th floor, Elephant House, 214 Broad Street.*

... and so it was that we took the first step towards the most difficult job of my life, restoring Lagos Island to its former glory.

Using the list of the members of ABOLI, I called them all to this inaugural meeting.

I was impressed that not only did they all come to the meeting, butthey also arrived punctually and with great enthusiasm.

Clearly, this was an issue that concerned the major stakeholders of Lagos Island.

It was indeed an impressive and formidable group:

- The United Africa Company (UAC)
- NOLCHEM, a wholly-owned subsidiary of Shell
- Shell Nigeria
- United Bank of Africa (UBA)
- First Bank of Nigeria (FBN)
- Union Bank
- International Bank for West Africa (IBWA)
- Shonny Investments and Properties Company(SIPC)
- The Cathedral Church on the Marina
- Legacy, headed by Professor John Godwin, an architect who had spent a lifetime in Nigeriaand was committed to preserving our historical legacies.
- Mrs Mosun Emeruwa, an architect and founder of the dynamic firm of architects, MOE

My message had resonated with all property owners, their tenants,and anyone who cared about this Island and were heartbroken by what was happening.

Our agenda was short and straight to the point

1. Self-Introduction
2. Self-Expressions
3. What are we going to do about it?

Once we had introduced ourselves, we quickly went to the next matter on the agenda.

Everyone was invited to describe the urban degradation in their neighbourhood of Lagos Island

The Central Business District (CBD) of Lagos Island, comprisingthe Marina and Broad Streets, was a long strip of land on two streets adjacent to each other, one of which, Marina, faced the Lagos Marina, the lagoon which traversed Lagos. It measures approximately 1.6 km long and 2.2 km wide.

Once the conversation started, there was no stopping them.

A ubiquitous comment from almost every participant was the question, "Gosh, I am surprised that you are the one initiating this meeting. Goodness, this end of Broad Street is the sanest."

There was the pathetic story of Union Bank, formerly Barclays Bank, who had just completed their 34-storey office block on the Marina, the tallest building in West Africa, if not Africa, at the time.

They were preparing to open this edifice with all the panachethey could muster, with their formidable array of international partners invited for the fiesta… But there was a problem.

Completely against every town planning norm in the world—andwe were to learn as we researched deeper into the wanton cause of the breakdown of law and order of the Lagos Island CBD, the local council had some of the most stringent rules and laws in the world—meat sellers, yes, meat sellers, had perched their stalls on the staircase leading to the entrance of this modern magnificent edifice.

Raw beef steaks, sirloin, tripe displayed in full view, with flies munching away, ready for sale!

Who cared that there were stringent laws, with penalties prohibiting the selling of any and all manner of meat outside the abattoirs?

Frustrated, Union Bank sent their officials to protest this flagrant infringement of the laws and breach of their rights as bona fide owners of the property to enjoy their development free of any menace or impediment.

The response from the Chairman of the Lagos Island Local Government, clearly on the take, was hilarious if it was not so outrageous.

He advised that Union Bank bring in and station fierce-looking dogs around their entrance. He assured them that not only were the meatsellers, like many Nigerians, terrified of dogs, but they would also be scared that the dogs would eat their meat!

That was their sincere counsel to the officials from Union Bank…And it worked.

First Bank regaled us with the tale that their entrance lobby, indeedthe whole of that side of Broad Street had been turned into smoked fish selling headquarters for all of Lagos. The fish were actually smoked in the public view, and you could be sure to get the very best assortment ofsmoked fish, and on occasion, bush meat.

Tinubu Fountain, the beautiful square which had been lovingly created by the Lebanese community and donated to Lagosians to mark our independence from the British in 1960, was now the headquartersof second-hand clothes sellers, where brisk business could be had in fullview of the glaring edifice of the Central Bank of Nigeria, adjacent to the magnificent head office of First Bank of Nigeria, and on and onit went. Filth generated from carelessly thrown peeled oranges, a must-have digestive with roasted plantain and peanuts, the favourite lunchtimesnack of very many white-collar managers and top officials who workedin the banks.

Utterly appalling, disgraceful filth all around.

And then, there was the menace of the Motor Park Union, a veritable mafia controlling the yellow Kombi buses, the official and mainmeans of transport for ingress and egress out of the island.

Even though there were clearly delineated bus lanes and parks, they had chosen to take them off the equation.

Although the buses had all been allotted specific routes to which they could pick passengers all over Lagos, this was too orderly and wouldnot pay the Motor Park Unions, and the enormous income they derived from the contrived chaos they had created.

All buses, no matter what route they were allotted, would congregate on Lagos Island and park at specific points, strategically selected (by Oke Arin Market) by CMS bookshop, from around noon, and effectively block the roads.

Going home on these buses was indeed the mayhem they had contrived.

The millions of workers that came into the Island from all the various neighbourhoods of Lagos Mainland had to negotiate their ways to enter the buses, and each passenger represented was a buck that wentto the pocket of the Motor Park Mafia.

We were moved to tears when we went around the once beautiful Marina gardens, the kilometres of space by the waterfront.

The Entrance Porch to Atlantic Hall

L-R Chief Mrs Keji Okunowo; Lady Gbeminiyi Smith;Chief Mrs Eniola Fadayomi; His Excellency, Vice President, Professor Yemi Osinbajo; me and Ladi

Cross section of Atlantic Hall Trustees andFriends, cutting the Celebration Cake at theSchool's 30th Anniversary

With His Excellency, Professor Yemi Osinbajo, at the30th Anniversary Celebration of Atlantic Hall

Receiving My Chieftaincy Title in 1989

With Muiz Banire at a LIMGE Strategy Meeting

With the First Bank of Nigeria (FBN)Representative, Mr Oshadiya

Mosun Ogunbanjo at a LIMGE Strategy Meeting

The Ajele Fire Station

The Fire Trucks delivered for the Ajele Fire Station

LAGOS ISLAND...

A City Reborn

Lagos Island; The Rebirth Agenda

With His Excellency, Former Governor Babatunde Fashola, at Lagos Island; The Rebirth Agenda

With Dr Stella Okoli, Mrs Ogunlesi, Dr K.O. Dinaand Chief Mrs Fadayomi, at Lagos Island; the Rebirth Agenda

L-R With Chief Mrs Marlies Allan and Chief MrsFadayomi, at Lagos Island; The Rebirth Agenda

Lanre Ogunlesi and I, at my 60th Birthday inBanjul

With Ladi at my 60th Birthday in Banjul

With Ladi and Our Sons, Olaleye and Ladipo

Pamela Watson and I

R-L Chief Mrs Eniola Fadayomi, Edith Fajemirokun, and I

With My Sister, Dr Stella Okoli, and myHusband, Ladi

L-R Ndidi Nwuneli; Joke Jacobs and I

L-R With Oba Otudeko, Alan Davies and KolapoLawson

With Pamela Watson and Andrew Jamieson, at theIdyllic Agaja Beach

Ann Pickard, Former Executive Vice President,Royal Dutch Shell

With Ladi and My Sister–in–Law, Dupe Ogunles

L-R Ladi, Dupe Ogunlesi, Me, and Lanre Ogunlesi, atDupe's 60th Birthday at Villa Eden, Merano, Italy

With My Beloved Late Daughter, Abioye Aronke Taiwo

FEAR ABIDES
WITH ME CONSTANTLY

INTIMATIONS OF FEAR AND MORTALITY

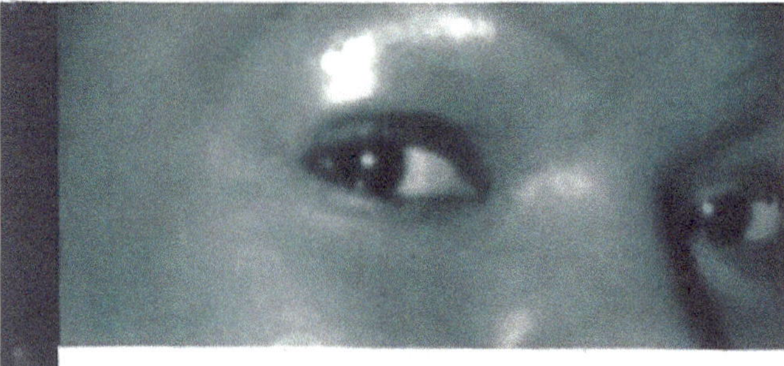

SCHOOL DAZE

HEARTH-STONE

KNOTS AND TANGLES

ABIOYE ARONKE TAIWO

edited by TONI KAN ONWORDI

Posthumous Book of Poems by Abioye Aronke Taiwo

With His Excellency, the Vice President, Professor Yemi Osin- bajo, at the International Aart of Life Foundation Symposiumin Abuja, titled "Setting an Agenda for The Future of Grief & Trauma Counselling in Nigeria"

L-R Dr Matthew Zack; Dr Femi Olugbile; Professor David Ndetei; Me; Dr Atilola; and Dr Daramola, at the International Aart of LifeFoundation Symposium in Abuja, titled "Setting an Agenda for The Future of Grief & Trauma Counselling in Nigeria"

L-R Me, Joke Jacobs, and Abiola Sanusi, at the International Aart of Life Foundation Symposium in Abuja, titled "Setting an Agendafor The Future of Grief & Trauma Counselling in Nigeria"

L-R Dr Mrs Stella Okoli, Me, Professor David Ndetei, and Dr FemiOlugbile, at the International Aart of Life Foundation Symposium in Abuja, titled "Setting an Agenda for The Future of Grief & Trauma Counselling in Nigeria"

My Mother

A veritable shantytown, with God knows how many people inhabiting the tin-roofed huts, all the better to pursue their nefarious activities on the Island.

We decided to label each shanty hut. We stopped when we reached 100.

The final assault was to the once-beautiful pride of Lagos Island, once romantically called The Marina Love Gardens, where young and not-so-young lovers could stroll and enjoy the soothing breeze of the marina.

There were the series of shipwrecks that littered the bay, doing God knows what damage to it.

It was generally believed that these ships were part of an international insurance scam. Ships supposed to be loaded for goods fordelivery at the Lagos Port of Apapa, opposite the marina waterfront, would be involved in some type of catastrophic accident and their wreckage deposited on the Lagos marina waterfront. It was said that millions of dollars were then claimed and collected on the insurance of the goods on the wrecked ships.

At any given time there were at least eight to ten of such wrecks littering the marina waterfront. They also no doubt were perfect hideouts and hangouts for the Lagos Island street urchins, gangsters now known by a ridiculously romantic name of Area Boys!

It felt good releasing all our pain, cathartic almost, and once every member of the group was done, an incredible sense of purpose was unleashed.

What next?

First things first, we decided that we needed to change the name of the original, initial founders from the Association of Building Ownersof Lagos Island (ABOLI). It was too restrictive, elitist, and exclusive. The problem on hand was grave. It posed an existential threat not only to the billions of Naira in investment by government and private investors, but the breakdown of law and order also jeopardised the health, wellbeing, and security of all inhabitants of Lagos Island.

We broke up into smaller committees, comprising:

- Law and Order
- Traffic and Congestion
- Urban Renewal and Beautification, and
- Preservation of Historical Monuments

Each committee was chaired by a member of the group and tasked with studying and coming up with a resolution of the committee they chaired and in which they had professional expertise.

Miss Mosun Ogunbanjo, a well-respected architect, chaired the committee on Urban Renewal and Beautification. Law and Order was chaired by Dr Fajemirokun, an astute lawyer. Traffic and Congestion was chaired by Mr Steve Mayaki, MD of UPDC. Preservation of Historical Monuments by Professor John Godwin, the renowned architect and head of Legacy.

I was to coordinate the group, and mount sustained pressure on Local, State and Federal Governments.

Within six weeks, we were to come back with our findings and move on with tackling the solutions.

Never doubt that a small group of thoughtful,
committed citizens can change the world; indeed, it'sthe
only thing that ever has.

— Margaret Mead

We came back six weeks later, and what a phenomenal amount ofdata our group of professionals had amassed.

We discovered, to the shock of all of us, that the Lagos Island Local Government had some of the most robust and stringent laws on every aspect of standard environmental laws, anti-social behaviour, andgeneral good neighbourliness in the world.

They had existing laws that banned spitting on the street! It was wide and all-encompassing, leaving nothing to the imagination.

The failure of enforcing these laws was simply due to the unwillingness of the local government authorities. And why, one may well ask? Gross corruption of unimaginable proportion, from the lowestclerk in the city council to the chairman of the local government.

We gasped in utter disbelief and pledged ourselves:

If we ever want to build or live in a Nigeria of our dreams, if we desire or envisage to enjoy the type of environment we so passionately desired, as leaders, we must involve ourselves in the communities in which we live. This was not an option, but an obligation.

Having earlier determined on our name, LIMGE, the first environmental pressure group consisting of concerned public-spirited citizens, property owners, tenants, and inhabitants of Lagos Island, came into being, convinced that a viable and successful metropolis of the new millennium is likely to be one that is run by governments and private stakeholders. We proceeded to set out our vision to make Lagos the 'Venice of Africa'… a viable, beautiful, and tourist-friendly city, where law and order reigns.

LIMGE's Mission:

> *To resolve, eradicate, through public-private partnerships, the major hazards of the Central Business District of Lagos Island, namely: traffic congestion, dilapidation of roads, lighting, street trading, homelessness, unemployment, inadequate sanitation, infrastructure, and air pollution.*

Our next steps involved mounting an aggressive and relentless campaign using the various media including TV interviews, printing press, radio et al.

We soon gained everyone's attention.

It was brought to our attention that what we were embarking on seemed extremely similar to what the business leaders of Cleveland, Ohio, had done some years ago when the city collapsed in a mountainof debt and refuse.

Their model had been studied and documented by the Harvard Business School, in their series, *Leadership in Action.*

To be honest, we were not aware of this study at the time but felt rather chuffed to discover that what we'd considered our original idea on how to save the city had been done before using a very similar model, which had been applauded by the Harvard Business School no less.

One of the most important lessons learnt by us from that study which we adopted was the importance of not trying to start by attemptinghuge projects, which would inevitably fail, and discourage members.

Our mantra was, 'Small victories lead to bigger victories.'

We set out very clear goals for ourselves to be achieved by a specific time.

They included:

- Sensitising, organising and mobilising the privatesector;
- Facilitating the relocation of Apongbon (underbridge bus stop) to eliminate traffic chaos;
- Facilitating routing of commercial vehicles;
- Donated one patrol van and towing vehicle and installation of Motorola radio system for traffic monitoring (donation by African Petroleum) to LASTMA;
- Street cleaning of Inner Marina for one year by Union Bank.

Very quickly, we caught the attention of the Lagos State Government with our strategic, relentless media campaign. The governorcalled us to a meeting at his office and, as I always did, I introduced ourpowerful list of formidable members.

First Bank, Union Bank, UBA, IBWA, UAC…

He stopped me before I could continue, saying, "The Owners of Lagos!"

"Yes, Your Excellency," I said, not missing a beat. "And we are no longer prepared to tolerate the breakdown of law and order on Lagos Island, watch our tenants terrified of being harassed and raped by gangsters."

My final *coup de grâce* always deliberately included some drama for special effects.

"When we invested the billions of Naira, which we all had done, in the CBD, we were not warned that government planned to abandon itand turn it into a rubbish dump. We want our money back!" I ended in the manner I had learnt from Margaret Thatcher.

Following a series of meetings with the different relevant government ministries, the governor of the day, His Excellency, Governor Tinubu—who without a doubt is one of the smartest, insightful visionaries we have ever had as Governor of Lagos despite his flaws (is there any amongst us without flaw?)—decided that this was a group the government should work with and together achieve our goals for a better Lagos.

We remained, unrepentantly, apolitical, but eagerly welcomed this opportunity.

We facilitated the establishment of a monthly forum, an advisory committee comprising LIMGE, the ministries of Environment and Physical Planning, Information, Youth and Sports, Works, Housing, Special Duties, Local Government Education, Nigerian Police,

Representatives of Oba of Lagos and Lagos Island.

A unique and never before conceptualised think-tank, where government would meet on a regular basis with top business leaders, share their vision, their limitations, and seek support of the private sector, and where leaders in the private sector would share their frustrations, point out areas where government policies were simply not working, brainstorm ideas together and come up with win-win solutions.

The private sector would act as government's eyes and ears on the beat, as it were, a veritable Public/Private partnership, with the ultimate aim of achieving our vision of making Lagos the 'Venice of Africa'...a viable, beautiful, tourist and business-friendly city, where law and order reign.

Below are some of LIMGE's achievements:

- Appealed to NEPA and achieved improved supply of electricity in Marina and Broad Streets. Our properties, all major high-rises, were charged commercial and industrial rates, astronomical rates between five to ten times higher than the residential buildings. A little arm twisting. We threatened to switch off our properties from NEPA, who said a little arm twisting gets you nowhere?
- Immediate positive reaction protected and prevented the unjustifiable arbitrary increases in tenement rates on Lagos Island.
- Facilitated the renovation of CMS bus stop by the Ministry of Works.

- Invitation to be part of the President's official delegation on his state visit to the United States of America in October 1999.
- Acceptance of LIMGE initiative by the Local, State, and Federal Governments.

In effect, playing a strategic carrot and stick hand, we became very quickly a formidable organisation that the government was obliged to reckon with.

Very early on it became apparent to us that something dramatic needed to be done about our non-existing firefighting or fire prevention capabilities of the moribund federal fire service.

The statistics were staggering. The fire service had never put outa single fire!

We found this appalling and decided to focus on this issue, makingit our pet project. We launched a major public awareness campaign to bring to light the utter abandonment of these essential services, using ournow time-tested strategy of discussion on the various media outlets, and relentlessly bringing the plight of the men and women who served in the fire brigade to the general attention of the horrified public.

We organised a well attended two-day Firefighting Workshop towards a fire safe city of Lagos with key stakeholders, and it culminated in a powerful communique which outlined major defects in the existing Fire Safety Act.

It led to the eventual revision of the Fire Safety Act, which included a provision that corporate bodies and individuals should establish mini fire services to support government efforts.

Ever conscious of our duty to show leadership and goodwill, LIMGE, through the sponsorship of its members Union Bank and First Bank, drilled a borehole at the Ajele Fire Station and it was commissioned on 28 October 2003 by Mr Jide Sanwo-Olu (the current Governor of Lagos State) who represented the Deputy Governor of Lagos State, Mr Femi Pedro, at the event.

This was followed by the construction of a 30,000-litre overhead storage tank at the Ajele Fire Station and the provision of uniforms for the rag tag men of the fire brigade, who were meant to risk their lives, confront raging fires without oxygen tents, uniforms, or even boots. Utterly disgraceful! Shame on all of us for standing by and allowing thisto go on for years. Shame on us.

We rounded off the year by completing the erection of two traffic lights at the junction of Broad Street by Odunlami Street as well as Broad Street by Kakawa Street using funds provided by our public-spirited member, First Bank of Nigeria.

Lagos State Commissioner for Transport, Alhaji Muiz Banire, commissioned the project on the same 28 October 2003.

We all relished that tremendous feeling of pride at our achievements. We had learnt the lesson so eloquently said and widely attributed to Mahatma Gandhi, *be the change you wish to see in the world.*

SPEAKING TRUTH TO POWER

We had established an advisory committee with the key arms of government. The very first of its kind, meeting monthly, sharing problems faced by governments in trying to execute their programs, and showing indisputable commitment on ourpart to step up, and assist the government in every way we could.

Government was well aware—the meetings were held in ouroffices in Elephant House—and if nothing else, it afforded them the opportunity to leave the Lagos State secretariat at Alausa, Ikeja, to witness in real time, the mass exodus from Lagos Island of many leadingcompanies and law-abiding citizens to escape the madness of the city. They were relocating to Victoria Island which had originally been zonedfor residential use, but was now a de facto commercial business district,leaving Lagos Island desolate, with empty buildings and scores of metresof vacant office space.

At a point in our eighteen-storey office block, Elephant House, allthe tenants had gone. I was left alone in the penthouse of the building with our few staff, surrounded by empty buildings to my right and left, gangsters and area boys running wild and terrifying the few people left in the neighbourhood, and, oh yes, then there were the humongous rats who now made the empty floors in the building their playground andwhat a field day they had of it.

Imagine if you would, and in the context that we held monthly advisory consultative meetings, our utter shock when we were all (members all of the advisory committee meetings with the key arms of government) served with notice of the Land Use Tax, and Lagos Island was selected to be the test case! How utterly blindsided we all were and utterly dismayed when we received, completely out of the blues, a notice that the Lagos State Government had decided to scrap tenement rates payable to the local government, merged it with two other taxes, neighbourhood (in a neighbourhood overrun by gangsters, mafia and rats!) and ground rent and created a new property tax, which they called the Land Use Tax.

The cost was staggering, and knowing as they very well knew, the situation of Lagos Island, with kilometres on kilometres of empty office space, dilapidated infrastructure, and the breakdown of law and order.

The proposed Land Use Act was staggering, for example ona building such as Elephant House, where tenants had all fled; they proposed the following:

Date of First Notice: Jan 04, 2002
Notice Number: 100000010681
Assessment Reference: ZRKIA41Q

ELEPHANT HOUSE BUILDING
214 BROAD STREET
LAGOS ISLAND, LAGOS
Delivery Code: 12687B-544712A2

Notice is hereby given in respect of the land and build-ing situated at the following location:
ELEPHANT HOUSE BUILDING **214 BROAD STREET** **LAGOS ISLAND, LAGOS**
The Land Buildings have been assessed in accordancewith the Land Use Charges Law, 2001 and have been found to have assessed Value as noted below:
₦1,090,989,000.00

The Land and buildings are being used for commercial purposes and are therefore subject to Land Use Charges of 1.75% of the assessed value. The following Land Use Charges are Payables.

For payment made between Feb 18, 2002 and Mar 05, 2002 pay this amount: ₦23, 865,384.38
For payment made between Mar 06, 2002 and Apr 05, 2002 pay this amount: ₦28, 638,461.25
For payment made between Apr 05, 2002 and May 04, 2002 pay this amount: ₦38, 184,615.00

The Lagos State Land Use Charges Law, 2001 requires that payment be made within thirty days of the date of this notice, meaning that payment is due on or before Feb 03, 2002 at any of the banks designated by Lagos State Government. If payment is made by Jan 19, 2002, the state and Local will accept a discounted amount of ₦ 16,228,461.38 as full payment of the Land Use Charges due for the year 2002.

The Lagos State Land Use Charges Law, 2001 provides for the penalties for delayed payment and these are fully enforceable and willbe enforced under the Law. The amount, including the penalties which will be payable in the event of payment delayed after the 15 days grace period following the due date above, is as follows.

Balance carried forward from previous land charges levelledby the state and the Local Government	Land Use Charges set for the Year 2002	Pay this Amount on dues date indicated
₦0.00	₦19,092,307.50	₦19,092,307.50

> *If payment in accordance with the foregoing is not received on or before May 04, 2002, the property to which this notice relates shall be liable to receivership by the State or its appointed agent until all outstanding taxes, payments, penalties, and administrative charges are paid underthe Law.*

The rates they were proposing to charge on these empty buildings, some of them in the case of Lapal House had not had a single tenant for over ten years when it was desolated by a major fire which could not be put out by our pathetic fire station and was razed to the ground.

To boot, the Land Use Tax was imposed on Lagos Island property owners only, as a test case!

We called an emergency meeting of the board; we were all truly upset. We decided to deal with the situation in a calm and reasonable manner.

We first sought a meeting with the legislators, as we felt they might not truly appreciate the depth of the situation. Despite spirited efforts, itwas simply impossible to meet with them. They froze us out!

Our colleagues on the advisory board had, likewise, frozen us out.

It was impossible to schedule a meeting with the governor.

A few months of being tossed around, we concluded that this was leading us nowhere. We decided to challenge the government in court. Surely, the government could not impose such a vexatious, illogical tax on its citizens that would be simply impossible to collect.

We wrote to every property owner on Lagos Island who had beensent this odious notice, informed them of our intention to challenge this vexatious law in the court, and asked them to join us in the legal challenge.

The result was truly remarkable.

Suddenly, membership in LIMGE tripled! Companies that had been on the sidelines of our struggle were now eager to be part of this dynamic movement. They paid the mandatory LIMGE membershipdues and also paid the obligatory contribution to the fees for the legal defence we were about to launch.

We engaged the services of a well-respected legal firm, Aelex, with its principal partner, Mrs Funke Adekoya, SAN. We had met on several occasions, and she had briefed us on the legal strategy they would be adopting.

We felt confident, and with the additional contributions of our new members to our legal challenge, we felt fully charged and ready to go, guns a-blazing.

Our first salvo was a full-page advert in *the Guardian Newspaper*, stating our position, in very clear and unambiguous terms:

THE LAGOS STATE LAND USE CHARGE ACT:
LIMGE (Lagos Island Millennium Group on the Environment)

Lagos Island Millennium Group on the Environment (LIMGE) is a not-for-profit which was established by concerned public-spirited citizens, property owners/tenants, and inhabitants of Lagos, who are disheartened by the disintegration and dilapidation of Lagos and determined to arrest the situation.

LIMGE's vision is to make Lagos the 'Venice of Africa'. A viable, beautiful, business, and tourist-friendly city, where Law and Order reign.

LIMGE is officially recognised by the Lagos State Government as an NGO that is working with the government to achieve this vision.

Many of its members own substantial commercial properties in Lagos. They have watched the billions of naira they invested in real estate in the city of Lagos go down the drain. Many of them are either unable to pay off the debts they incurred in constructing these buildings or realise the return on their enormous investment in the city of Lagos.

Presently, there are floors and floors of vacant office space in Metropolitan Lagos, with many businesses fleeing the dilapidation of social infrastructure, filth, and squalor of the Central Business District of Lagos.

Members of LIMGE are appalled that the Lagos State Government, instead of taking appropriate action to tackle the above problem, and without adequate consultation, has proceeded to enact the vexatious and ill-conceived law that is the "LAND USE CHARGE LAW".

LIMGE members are equally astonished that in this era of democracy, members of the Lagos House of Assembly have apparently sanctioned the enactment of such a hostile, high-handed and arrogant law.

The Law is riddled with inconsistencies. It appears to have calculated and based its assessment of tenement rates on its assessor's capricious and whimsical valuation of properties. It fails to take into consideration voids in buildings, rental value and the ability of the owners and their tenants to pay.

As a result, building owners are being asked to pay tenement rates on properties where there are no tenants. Others are asked to pay an annual rate up to 1000% higher than the annual rent receivable etc. Then there is the unconstitutional proviso that 50% of these outrageous rates be paid first, before seeking to appeal.

Lagos Island Millennium Group on the Environment (LIMGE) at its General Meeting of Members, which was held on the 26th of September, 2001, resolved not to pay this Vexatious Tax.

Meanwhile, LIMGE is conferring with its Lawyers and will advisemembers on appropriate legal action being taken within the shortest possible time.

LIMGE is committed to its Mission and Vision of making Lagos "A VIABLE BEAUTIFUL BUSINESS AND TOURIST-FRIENDLY CITY, WHERE LAW AND ORDER REIGN".

SIGNED,

EXECUTIVE COMMITTEE (LIMGE)

Chief Mrs T.I. Taiwo - MD, Shonny Investments & Properties Co. Ltd., President

Mr S. Mayaki - MD, UACN Property & Dev. Co., 1st Vice President
Mr A. Olufon - MD, Afribank Estate Ltd., 2nd Vice President

B. Oshadiya (First Bank of Nigeria Plc) Mr Aseweje (Wemabod Estates) Ambassador O. Adesola

Mrs Y. Ogunsulire -Ismail (National Bank)Dr H. Sanni (Union Bank Plc.)

Mr Godwin (Godwin & Hopwood Architects)

Mr O.J. Lawson (Ub40 Ltd.)

– The Guardian, 14 November 2001

I was not at all fearful of the wrath of the government and proudly signed my name as President of LIMGE, as did most of the members of the board.

Every member of the board was shown the draft of the letter, with some adding additional points. I had no doubt we had a complete meeting of the minds and agreement on a sense of purpose…or so I thought.

On Friday evening, can I ever forget that evening? I received a call from one of our key board members who was nodding her head in total agreement to the tone of the letter that is until she asked the question: "Whose signature is on the letter?" "All our board members," I replied.

She screamed, "Taiwo, don't tell me my name is on the letter!" She was now hysterical. "How can you put my name on the letter? *I ampursuing a large payment from Lagos State, and this will seriously jeopardise my ability to collect my money.*"

She was beyond hysterical, I calmed her down assuring her that I would ensure that her name was removed from the advertorial.

I immediately called my friend, Lady Maiden Ibru, Chairman of *Guardian Newspapers*, and pleaded with her to ensure that the advertorial we had placed and was scheduled to come out on Monday was kept on hold.

I then called an emergency LIMGE board meeting. I very dramatically demanded to know if other lily-livered board members were unwilling to put their names on a petition that we had all agreed upon.

I told them emphatically that I was not chasing any contract in Lagos State, did not harbour any political ambitions, and was proud to put my name on a cause I was passionate about. What we could not afford was to place an advert and then have members disassociating themselves from it. That would be disastrous.

To my delight, one by one, they all said in unison, "Put my name on the advert."

I think my reputation amongst our members grew in leaps and bounds that day and is why I continue to enjoy tremendous goodwill amongst all the top business leaders of Lagos Island till today.

I was later informed that the Governor of Lagos was livid with usand especially with me!

I have no political ambition, never had and never shall, did not do business with the government, but I was very much aware that fighting the government, in such an open manner was a perilous affair. I was alsoaware that if we did not stop this vexatious act before it gained traction,the fate of all property owners of Lagos was doomed.

Ultimately, after some wrangling, it was decided that the matter would best be settled out of court, and we ultimately reached an amicable consensus, restructuring the weak, illogical basis on which the Law was based, an imaginary value of buildings which they had not even bothered to enter, irrespective of whether it was occupied or not and other such illogical premises.

Following the advertorial, our lawyers formally commenced the legal proceeding against the Land Use Act on behalf of LIMGE.

A red-letter day for LIMGE and Lagosians.

Lagos State saw the lack of merit in the manner in which this taxation had been promulgated and it was mutually agreed that the matter is settled out of court.

A new substantially reduced Land Use Act was promulgated.

Property Classification	Old Rates	New Rates
Commercial Property	1.75%	0.375%
Residential property/ commercial	0.65%	0.65%
Industrial premises of Manufacturing Concerns	0.50%	0.125%
Owner Occupied Residential Property	0.15%	0.375%
Owner Occupied Pensioner's Property	EXEMPT	EXEMPT
Family Compound/Public ETC	EXEMPT	EXEMPT

The new rates will be applicable for a period of seven years commencing from the 1st of January, 2002.

In effect, all bills for 2002 have now been discounted by 75% or more, depending on the class of the property in question.

For the property owners who, by virtue of the recalculation of therates for 2002, have now overpaid their Land Use Charge for 2002, a credit of overpayment will be made toward future Land Use Charges.

The current valuations made under the Land Use Charge No. 11 of 2001 shall not be unreasonably increased in the future. All proposals for review shall be taken in conjunction with Independent Registered Estate Surveyors and Valuers.

For all defaulting property owners, including those who have paida portion of their Land Use Charge for 2002, full settlement of the amount due under the revised rates outlined in paragraph 7 is payableon or before 30 April 2003.

For clarity, a letter indicating either the amount of credit orbalance due and payable on account will be issued by the Lagos State Commissioner for Finance.

Notice advising property owners to the assessment for Land Use Charge Rate 2003 will be issued in due course and these notices will show Land Use Charges for each property based on the reductions outlined above in this public notice.

In spite of a judicial pronouncement by a court of competent jurisdiction that the Land Use Charge Law No. 11 2002 is valid and constitutional, the government is also working on a Bill for the amendment of some portions of the Law, including the penalty section, in response to suggestions received from property owners. There will befull consultation with all stakeholders, including the Organized Private Sector, during this process.

The Organized Private Sector shall withdraw all court actions instituted to challenge the Land Use Charge Law and shall use its best endeavour to get its members to do likewise.

Signed by the Honourable Commissioner for Information and Strategy, Lagos State.

I wonder how many Lagosians know that if it was not for this courageous act of LIMGE, they might well have been burdened by this ridiculous law, which would have inevitably led to many property companies going bankrupt!

We decided to take LIMGE to another level and set up a vision forthe next five years.

And on the heels of a new election for another new government, we organised a unique strategic planning workshop, LAGOS VISION 2007, for the incoming governments, business leaders, and other stakeholders,to create a common vision for all stakeholders.

In addition and to gain insights from international experts from cities who are dealing or have dealt with some of the challenges being faced by the city of Lagos, four environmentalists were invited from Egypt, Brazil, South Africa, and Spain.

We are ever appreciative of The Institute of International Education in New York through the Ford Foundation for making this possible by giving us a grant for the Vision 2007 Program.

The two-day workshop which was brilliantly facilitated by IFP Limited, ICAI Associates, Nigerian Facilitators Network, and the Institute of Education was well attended, with a varied and eclectic group of leaders from all arms of government, the private sector, Lagos royalty, the academia, various NGOs, religious leaders, and World Bank representatives.

At the end of what can only be described as a one-of-a-kind event,the group agreed on a Vision 2007 for Lagos Island, Eti-Osa Local Government, and Lagos State Government. It set out our aspirations of what we wanted to achieve within the next five years of their term, and committed to support the government achieve these goals.

We came up with a vision of our aspirations for thenext four years:

- world class entertainment recreational culturalfacilities
- free movement of people and vehicles
- good leadership
- well-planned neighbourhoods
- clean environment
- effective security system
- excellent public utilities.
- they also identified the following obstacles todelivering the vision
- poor policy formulation and implementation
- poor maintenance culture
- corruption on all fronts

- anti-social attitudes
- acute poverty
- poor financial management

We decided to pursue the following strategic directionsto achieve the vision which included:

- selling the vision
- encouraging community involvement
- funding the vision
- promoting transparency, openness and accountability
- creating gainful employment
- promoting efficient service delivery
- building capacity
- eliminating corrupt practices

We agreed on a 12-month implementation plan, set upthree task forces to achieve specific targets during the first 90days with the following sub goals:

1. Selling the vision and creating awareness
2. Data collection
3. Rehabilitation of area boys
4. All participants agreed to pursue the vision with vigour while enlisting all stakeholders to achieveit

Undoubtedly, this remarkable two-day workshop set in motion the tremendous success achieved by LIMGE in the years that followed.

We sent a bound copy of the workshop and its goals to the LagosState Government, the president of the federation, every single state government and every stakeholder and funding agency we could think of.

We printed 400 copies of this document and sent out a good 300 odd to all the above plus more.

We held press interviews and were aggressive in our aim of selling the vision.

It worked. Indeed, so very well that His Excellency, Tinubu, then Governor of Lagos State, who was approaching the end of his term, bought so deeply into the vision that he called it his own.

He launched Lagos Island Rehabilitation Programme which included all the features we had in our vision. As we set about to commence the Area Boys rehabilitation programme, having worked vigorously in collaboration with Fate Foundation and DIN and using as a prototype a model adopted from Porto Alegre town in Brazil (which had successfully integrated the street urchins and gangsters), raised funds from a French agency to execute the programme, secured their training in vocational programs, carefully selected, with a panel which included psychiatrists, chairman of the LGA and other professionals, the initial candidates we were to admit into the programme.

We had secured a property in Epe where we were to commence the programme. Ready to go, alas we were once again blindsided by a much-publicised announcement by the Lagos State Government that they were launching a massive Area Boys' rehabilitation programme in Ita-Oko, Ajah-Lekki, Lagos State, which would accommodate hundredsof these youth urchins.

Many of our members were livid, indeed, the press in attendance at that meeting questioned the state government if they were not copyingthe project that LIMGE was about to launch?

My attitude was honestly different, the greatest compliment one can give is to copy your idea, lock, stock and barrel.

Was it frustrating that we had put so much into conceptualisinga workable scheme, convinced our corporate members to employ the reformed boys once they had gone through the programme and been certified, raising the French funding? Naturally, it was frustrating, butI chose to console myself that, we had in effect achieved something to be proud of, we got government to do their job, and that can never bea bad thing. It was so sad to learn later that there was no rehabilitation programme. All the street urchins had simply been rounded up and sent to an island-like jail, which if rumour is to be believed, was surrounded by crocodiles!

THE CBD REBIRTH AGENDA

On 29 May 2007, Mr Babatunde Fashola SAN, was inaugurated as the new governor of Lagos State.

He was the former Chief of Staff to Governor Ahmed Tinubu, and there was every indication that he was going to continue his revolutionary policies.

Indeed, Governor Ahmed Tinubu, in spite of natural human flaws,had achieved some remarkable success in Lagos State during his eight- year rule; innovative, forward-looking and sometimes simply remarkable.

We were eager to continue our work on Lagos Island and achieveour aims as was set out in our Vision 2007 proclamation. As soon ashe was able to grant us an audience, we scheduled a meeting with our executives. After the usual pleasantries, he dug straight at us:

"LIMGE, you folks are more famous for challenging governmentthan anything else." He went on, "Why don't you demonstrate your prowess by doing something really big for Lagos?"

He went on to tell us that the Federal Government had handed over the federal fire services to Lagos State, and then, he threw us a challenge:

"Why don't you build a world class fire station in Lagos...? You will forever be celebrated."

According to him, the government had an urgent need for more patrol vans to beef up the security of the neighbourhood, and concludedthat to change the mindset of our indigenes, we needed to have a massivepublic awareness campaign to educate the masses on sanitation, pollution, and traffic management.

Part of the challenge was to provide security in the Central Business District (CBD), and immediately after the meeting, Union Bank purchased five (5) patrol vans for Lagos Island. We delivered them to the Commissioner for Transportation at the Lagos Government Headquarters.

A special tool was designated for communication between tradersand visitors, including tourists, detailing what can and cannot happenin the Central Business District (CBD). This tool also contained factual maps of the CBD.

First Bank of Nigeria donated the sum of twenty-eight million naira (₦28 million) to LIMGE, to execute a six-month campaign. But in the first instance, whilst distributing thousands of copies of this invaluable, much sought-after street finders, long before the advent of GPS, companies placed adverts in the pocket-sized maps of the CBD, and the project was a huge success.

Many corporate bodies signed on to the project, and their business locations were highlighted in the legend, giving their business and branch network better visibility.

Governor Fashola perhaps did not realise this, but he had selected areas LIMGE was passionate about. Indeed, they formed part of our Vision 2007 Agenda.

We left his office and went straight to work.

Working with a first-class marketing and PR company, Connect Marketing, and its boss, the self-effacing but ever so smart Tunji Adeyinka, and Temi, we developed the marketing and fundraising document we titled 'LAGOS ISLAND… A City Reborn'.

UNFORGETTABLE FRIENDS

I had made firm friends with Pamela Watson and her partner, Andrew Jamieson, with his killer sense of humour. I had an open invitation tojoin them at their beach hut in the idyllic Island of Agaja, a 45-minute ride on a speed boat from Lagos.

Even the ride through the mangroves on both sides of the Lagoon foretold that something out of this world lay ahead of us. Gradually, we could see the outline of the most beautiful Island…and then, you would see it emerge. Behold Agaja, in all its majesty, a small strip of land sandwiched between the Lagoon and the Atlantic Ocean.

The first time I spent the night with my friends, Pamela and Andrew, at Agaja—dining with candlelight by the beach, listening to reggae music, and then, going up the rickety stairs where there was another sitting area, watching the spectacular view of the Lagoon with palm trees draped intermittently like a shawl, sipping our coffee, totallylost in the stunning beauty as we gazed at the moon shining brightly, accentuating the staggering beauty of it all—I was jolted back to earth by a phone call from my home in Lagos.

"Taiwo, where the hell are you?" my brother-in-law asked.

"I am in heaven," I replied without missing a beat. *She's lost it*, he probably thought.

Truly, a night stay in Agaja was the nearest thing to heaven on earth I had ever experienced.

I never missed an opportunity to join Pamela and Andrew on every occasion I was invited, and it became a weekly ritual.

There were other fascinating people who had beach huts in Agaja, mostly the expatriate heads of multinational organisations who made this idyllic island their pothole to unwind. And what an amazing time we had of it.

Great barbecues—more like a gastronomic delight fit for Henry VIII—scintillating conversation, I loved the one-hour nap I always took on the hammock, lulled to sleep by the gentle breeze off the Atlantic Ocean. Heaven.

Agaja was a unique place to make great friends of the top executives whose companies all owned beach huts there.

Andrew, Pamela's husband, was the Managing Director of Nigeria Liquefied Natural Gas (NLNG). He was seconded to the position from Shell, who held a 25.6% stake in NLNG.

I met Ann Pickard at Agaja, and we became firm friends. Ann was the Executive Vice President of Shell in Africa. A very powerful and influential lady indeed.

On one of our many trips to Agaja, I told her about our ambitious project of building a first-class fire station at Ajele, equipped to world class standards, and training a hundred-man squad kitted to world-class standards. She was fascinated by the idea.

It just happened that Ajele Fire Station was right next door to Shell's nineteen-storey head office. They were deadly aware of the perilous situation Lagos was in without a functioning fire station nor trained and equipped firemen.

We submitted the proposal to Shell, and I was blown away when, without the usual crippling decision-making process those types of CSR initiatives usually took, I received the letter that Shell had approved our proposal for the construction of a new fire station equipped to the best standards in the world, and a hundred-man squad to be trained by a team of firemen from New York.

I walked on air. We did it, we did it, we did it! Shell confirmed the approval of the sum of two million dollars ($2,000,000).

A purpose-built storey building was handed over to the AjeleFire Station on Monday, 2 December 2013, with Mr Jolaoso, Deputy Comptroller-General of the Federal Fire Service standing in for his boss who was indisposed. The new fire station, which has been added to the Centenary Projects, boasts:

- A state-of-the-art fully equipped and functional fire service, dedicated to businesses within the Central Business District and beyond, accessible 24hrs, and capable of dealing with fire in a twenty-storey building;

- A fully equipped mobile security force maintaining law and order, with direct access to the police in cases of extreme security threats;
- A team of hundred well-trained fully-kitted firemen on the ready at all hours, who attended a comprehensive and extensive two (2) weeks training facilitated by the Fire Chief from the New Jersey Fire Department, USA; and
- Brand new firefighting kits, and a full complement of top quality, modern firefighting and communication equipment, the best available in the world

Not so fast. I was to later learn, to my chagrin and constellation, nothing ever works seamlessly with the government.

We learnt the staff employed by the Federal Government had much better salary and conditions of service, and refused to be transferred to Lagos State to become employees of the State Government.

And so, they went on strike!

This strike went on for at least six months, and was only called off when they were assured they would not be transferred to the services and employment of Lagos State Government.

It began to dawn on me that it appeared there was no plan for the advancement of Nigeria, only a plan to shred it into a carcass.

Could it be that I had been naive all long? That it really was not possible to change my world even if I put my guts, my passion, into the effort?

We soldiered on. It was explained to us that anyone who worked for the Federal Government, with its infinitely better conditions of services, would be foolish to allow themselves to be downgraded, as it were, to employment with a State Government.

We had decided we would build a brand-new block, modelled to world-class standards. We discovered the design for fire stations were basically similar worldwide. Their requirements were identical.

We engaged the services of a very pleasant and utterly professional architect, Taiwo Oyeleke, of Triarch Construction, to carve out the new Ajele Fire Station from the site of the headquarters of the fire brigade stationed at Ajele.

We were emphatic, our brief was not to contribute to the construction of the headquarters of a paramilitary federal institution such as the Federal Fire Station, no matter that it was in a serious state of disrepair.

We assembled a committee of professionals and asked Shell to nominate their top fire engineer and his team to be integral membersof the committee. The team had been responsible for the constructionof Shell Fire Station in Port Harcourt, and they were considered their specialists.

We were also determined that the process would not only be scrupulously professional and above board, we believed that having key Shell staff on the team would provide the necessary oversight.

We met weekly and carried out the task in front of us in a very professional and open manner.

Integrity, accountability and timeliness, were my buzz words, andwe ran the project under those strict guidelines.

The contributions of Engineer Fasanmi and his boss, Raymond, were invaluable.

The first bottleneck we encountered to our shock was getting the requisite approval from Lagos State Ministry of Physical Planning for the construction of the project.

I was jaw droppingly flabbergasted to learn that almost ninemonths later, some officials in the ministry were deliberately frustratingour effort to obtain an approval to build a first-class fire station to be donated to Lagos State and its inhabitants.

I was hopping mad.

I stormed the offices of the top official in the department, with our team from Shell in tow, in a rage. I told them it would be my pleasure having raised the money for the project, to return it back to Shell and expose the reason why!

My melodramatic scene had the desired effect, and we obtained the approval almost immediately thereafter.

16 February 2010 was another red-letter day. The committeehad picked that date randomly, unaware it was my birthday, to plan the turning of the soil ceremony which was to be performed by the Federal Minister of Internal Affairs, under whose ministry was the Fire Brigade.

I reminded members of the committee that the day was my birthday, and told them that whatever they had in mind, they should remember I had a twin sister.

A brief but joyous ceremony it was. The minister mentioned he had not been to Lagos since he left Lagos University decades ago, but hewas simply blown away by our extraordinary public spiritedness, to haveraised money to build a first-class fire station for Lagosians.

The committee had organised two beautiful birthday cakes, one for me and the other for my twin sister.

I was sad to note that she did not show up.

The Ajele Fire Station was run in an extremely professionalmanner. Guiding us in the background was Mr Mallije Okoye.

The team of professionals who attended our weekly meetings held throughout the execution of the Project included fire specialist engineers who worked with us on a committee, Engineer Fasanmi and his boss, Engineer Raymond, who were the top fire specialists in Shell, and invaluable members of the board of LIMGE.

Arc Taiwo Oyeleke's company of architects and builders was recommended by Shell. We had signed a turnkey contract with them, and they were able to get on with the project with only the occasional sitevisit to view landmarks, as per the agreed contract.

We completed the project on time and delivered the following:

- A new one-storey building, a functional, state-of-the-art fire service station;
- The building was fully furnished with training rooms, a fully equipped gym. In addition to the offices and lounge, ithad a small hostel with beds, recognising that firemen are human and need, on occasion, to rest between emergencycalls;

- A 45 KVA generator set;
- In the lobby was a television, whilst we provided top quality firefighting communication equipment;
- Oxygen masks and enough supply of oxygen for twelve months; and
- The *pièce de résistance*: 4 BMW firefighting motorcycles to enable our squad to enter the notorious narrow nooks and corners of Lagos Island

What joy to see the look of pride on all their faces, wearing their uniforms, extremely proud to call themselves firemen of the LIMGE squad?

Our project completed, we took the Shell Nigeria Exploration and Production Company (SNEPCO) management on a tour of the building, accompanied by their charming CEO, Chike Onyejekwe.

We had a plaque displayed prominently in the lobby:

WORLD CLASS AJELE FIRE STATION

DELIVERED

A PROMISE MADE. A PROMISE KEPT

MADE POSSIBLE BY THE GENEROUS DONATION OF SHELL

That, or so we thought, was the end of the matter. I was also looking forward to receiving an award for putting together and handing over such a phenomenal project for the benefit of all Lagosians.

I was sadly mistaken.

We kept writing, first to the Lagos State Governor, inviting him to the commissioning—No response—then we tried the Federal Ministry of Internal affairs through the Comptroller-General, Mr Okebiorun, we were naive enough to believe what we had achieved wasso phenomenal the Head of State, President Goodluck Jonathan, would be happy to commission the landmark project, if nothing else, to thank us and demonstrate to Nigerians what public-spirited individuals could achieve—Silence.

Meanwhile, we had engaged the services of a cleaner to ensure the place was kept maintained to our standards.

Utterly unbelievable. The fire brigade had, without our permission, connected their head office, which we had given a perfunctory tidying up to align a little with the newly-built Ajele Fire Station, to the generator set, and went as far as to ask us to buy some more diesel when they exhausted what was provided for the station.

We made it clear that Ajele Fire Station was built to provide support to businesses and inhabitants of Lagos in the event of a fire outbreak, and certainly not to support the headquarters of a paramilitary organisation such as the Federal Fire Brigade.

No response.

The back and forth went on for a good six months, leaving me hopelessly deflated and confused. Again, I came to the sad conclusion that our leaders really had no plans for Nigeria, or worse, self-interest, greed, and whatever else it was that ailed them, had made them willy- nilly complicit in the destruction of our beloved Nigeria.

I was saddened beyond words.

One fine day not long after this, I was delighted when I received acall from the offices of the governor of Lagos State. I recall it well. It wasa Friday, and I was informed His Excellency had accepted our invitationto commission and take over our ultra-modern Ajele Fire Station.

Only problem was he scheduled the handover for Monday. We had two days' notice, a Saturday and Sunday!

I quickly informed all our members and invited the Minister of Internal Affairs to the event.

I was speechless when I received a message back from the Federal Minister of Internal Affairs that the Governor of Lagos State dare not come to commission Ajele Fire Station as it was on federal government property. He went on.

He had given strict instructions that should he dare come, his menhad been ordered to block him out and ensure he and his entourage would not be allowed to set foot inside the compound.

I discussed with the team and decided we must immediatelycancel the scheduled visit and commissioning by the Governor of LagosState. The humiliation of such a disgraceful drama was too much to contemplate.

I must say to the credit of Governor Fashola, that he was extremely gracious about the whole thing.

We rescheduled the event for the next day, a Tuesday, givingus enough time to invite the top executives of Shell, led by the ever- charming

Managing Director, Mr Chike Onyejekwe, our LIMGE members, members of the various boards on which I sat, family and friends. The Deputy Comptroller-General of the fire brigade arrived to represent the Minister of Internal Affairs.

We gave them all a guided tour of the facilities, our LIMGE fire squad kitted with their new firefighting gear. We showed off a bit by getting the trained riders in full motorcycle gear, boots and all, to ride their BMW firefighting motorcycles around the neighbourhood.

They were all blown away. I was surrounded by a sea of people congratulating us heartily.

"How on earth were you able to pull this off, Taiwo?"

I looked around and noted sadly that once again, my twin sister was not there.

Well, we never did get an award from either the Lagos State or federal government to this day. We did not even receive a thank you letter.

We nevertheless relished the sense of achievement and knowledge we had demonstrated that as business leaders, if we wanted to makea positive change in our country, we must involve ourselves in our community. This is not an option, but an obligation.

Alas, I found that God was not done with me yet. He had putin my destiny, another task. This time, the most heart-breaking, heart-wrenching one imaginable.

BEAUTIFUL 'BIOYE AND THE AART FOUNDATION

When I am at my most destroyed, I am about to grow.

My daughter, Abioye Aronke Taiwo, 'Bioye, as she was fondlyknown, returned to Nigeria in December 2001, after ten yearsof studying and living in England. She graduated in 1998 with honours in Law and Literature from the University of Staffordshire.She completed her legal practitioner's course as a solicitor in 1999, and had been a practicing solicitor in the UK before her return. Born in Omaha, Nebraska, USA, on 3 December 1977, she was very proud of her American passport.

Beautiful, sensitive, kind, and compassionate. She was down-to-earth, humble, and always, always, herself. She was always on a questto discover new ways of being and new creative possibilities. When shegot tired of what she perceived as the shallow and facile style of new Hollywood movies, she took to watching black and white avant-garde French films.

For her young years, her insightful understanding of the meaning and purpose of life was extraordinary. 'Bioye was a talented singer and poet who loved to cook. From a very early age, she would say, "I am goingto be a famous poet one day."

'Bioye was also flirtatious, funny, sassy, and ambitious. After years of studying and living in England, which she loved, she decided to broaden her horizons by moving to New York in June 2001. In the threemonths she spent there, she came to love it, made many new friends, anddecided she would return to sit for the New York Bar Exams in January2002.

Then came 9/11. Instead of the New York Bar Exams, home beckoned, and she opted for the Nigerian Law School instead. Ten years after leaving Nigeria, she returned home, and we were all delighted to have her back with us.

Through her ability to get along with different kinds of people, 'Bioye quickly adapted to Nigeria and made new friends.

She declined the opportunity to spend an extra week with friends and family during a short break in London that Easter, and instead, cameback to Lagos on 11 April 2002. Again, she declined another opportunityto accompany me, her mother, her best friend, and her great travelling companion, on what was evidently going to be an exciting study trip to Cairo.

"I can't go gallivanting around the world with you, Mummy dearest," was how she put it. "I'm in Nigeria to attend Law School and pass. I have to make up for the notes I missed during the Easter break."

Catching up on her notes was exactly what 'Bioye was doing that fateful Friday, 19 April 2002, having firmly declined all offers to go out that evening. But then, two of her friends from the Nigerian Law School came calling at around 10:30 p.m. that evening. She was somehow convincedto get into the car with them. She left her laptop on, her bottle of water, her notes, suggesting she had no intention of going far. Two minutes later, as they were about to cross the notorious, dark, unlit intersection of Sobo Arobiodu Street, Mobolaji Bank-Anthony Way, a lorry crashedinto the rear of the car in which she was a passenger. 'Bioye was killed onthe spot, being the only fatality in the accident. With this, the incrediblepromise of her life seemed extinguished. We were stunned by her death.It unleashed a wave of grief amongst people all over Nigeria and friendsfrom all over the world, many of whom had never met her. 'Bioye, aged24, had clearly touched so many people's lives.

I recall seeing my mother's heartbroken face when I walked downthe stairs of my house the very first time since receiving the life-changing news. Her eyes blood-red with tears, the first time in my life I had ever seen her cry. Her sense of guilt was palpable. It was a mirror image of mine.

"My husband, I failed. How could I not have prevented this from happening? I am your mother. It is my duty to have protected you from such a heart-breaking tragedy." The exact same primordial mother's angst I was feeling about my darling 'Bioye. Heartrending guilt, extremerage, and paralysing fear.

One of the most difficult aspects of 'Bioye's sudden and premature departure was the thought that her twenty-four years in the world would be obliterated, that in a couple of years, people might not remember her. They might wonder if she ever existed or if she was a phantom or afigment of their imagination. I simply could not live with that notion. I obsessed over that for a while. I did not want her memory to dissolve withthe dust. *I cannot, and I will not, forget Abioye Aronke Taiwo*.

With that in mind, I came up with the vision for the Aart of Life Foundation. The Abioye Aronke Taiwo Way of Life Foundation: living for good to do good!

I thank God that through the foundation—and its ground-breaking achievements of the last eighteen years, in road safety awareness, grief and bereavement counselling, and youth development—I have watched Abioye Aronke Taiwo bloom and grow in this world. I have been her voice in the last eighteen years. I am proud that the world has listened and heard, and will continue to hear her.

I emptied myself and healed my broken soul.

Aims & Objectives of the Foundation

The Aart of Life Foundation was established in September 2002 with thisoverall purpose, to "promote and advance the virtues of love, kindness, compassion, charity, beauty, and sensitivity, amongst all Nigerians, and especially amongst Abioye's generation." Under this broad charter, the objectives of the foundation are to:

- Promote individualism amongst young people
- Provide Grief/Trauma Counselling support services to Nigerians in their time of grief/trauma

- Provide one-on-one counselling support centres
- Encourage soul consciousness and an appreciation of the meaning and purpose of life

The Aart of Life pioneering initiative in grief/trauma counselling (the first-ever in Nigeria) has, in the eighteen years of its inauguration, had an enormous impact on the lives of the bereaved and those experiencing trauma.

It is helping to break cultural taboos in discussing death and bereavement, by underscoring the absence of organised social support in Nigeria, and drawing attention to the urgent need to make these unique services available to Nigerians, especially to those who are poor or bereaved. Mourning had hitherto been characterised by displays of grief,including constant attention from friends and relatives for a ritualised period. Damaging widowhood rights are still practised, and taboos around mental illness limit people's willingness to discuss their grief andseek help.

The Aart of Life Foundation has offered grief counselling in the English language to an estimated two thousand Nigerians from all walks of life. Nigeria is diverse in ethnicity, religion and language, with over two hundred and fifty ethnic groups and over five hundred languages and dialects (www.ng.undp.org/mdgs/Final-MDGreport-2010). However, three ethnic groups of Yoruba, Hausa and Igbo, are dominant, and their languages, the most spoken in Nigeria. The Foundation is planning to increase our reach by including these three indigenous languages.

In 2009, in partnership with Lagos State University Teaching Hospital (LASUTH), we trained and certified twenty grief counsellors in three states. We have trained up to three hundred and fifty grief counsellors, and have recently selected eighty more to be trained and certified to help Nigerians in their time of grief and trauma. We maintaina register of trained counsellors and continue to offer a toll-free grief and trauma counselling service.

We are extremely proud of this ground-breaking, pioneering initiative in this field, and of our numerous achievements. We are enormously conscious of the tremendous need and ever-increasing demand of our compatriots in this increasingly complex world for grief and trauma counselling across Nigeria.

The need is so much greater than what we can offer without scalingup our services. In 2019, in a country with a population of nearly 200 million, an estimated 2.3 million Nigerians died.

Australian research suggests that each death leaves in its wake five bereaved people, of whom 6% suffer chronic and disabling grief. These figures will be higher in Nigeria, reflecting more untimely deathsfrom accidents, terrorism and high maternal and child mortality rates, lack of social and counselling services and unhelpful cultural taboos andpractices. Thus, we conservatively estimate 11.6 million Nigerians are grieving a death each year, of whom 700,000 suffer chronic and disabling grief and need specialist bereavement care.

In 2020, coronavirus is increasing the death rate and the numbersof chronical, disabled bereaved people to even higher levels. Nigeria has confirmed a total of 22,020 coronavirus cases and recorded 547 deaths in the three months since the first case was recorded.

The epidemic of those chronically bereaved is every bit as disabling and tragic as the coronavirus pandemic now afflicting our country. On top of this, it was estimated in 2017 that there were only 130psychiatrists in Nigeria and over 20 million Nigerians suffering mental illness. Many Nigerians, unable to access any form of psychiatric supportor counselling, turn to traditional healers. The Nigerian government hasnot made mental healthcare a priority and only 3% of the health budget goes to mental healthcare; there is a massive vacuum of support thatmust be taken up by private foundations like Aart of Life.

Aart of Life is at the forefront of the work to support the bereaved,but the task is huge. We need to ramp up, to get the support of the government, the private sector and international partners to deploy our innovative grief counselling training and hotlines, and to develop other services, especially those leveraging mobile telephony and technology, to extend our beneficial impact.

Partnerships

Aart of Life Foundation in partnership with Lagos State University Teaching Hospital (LASUTH), and Lagos State Ministry of Health (LSMTH), developed a unique four-stage approach to grief and trauma counselling which achieved tremendous success in Nigeria. The training was divided into four methods to achieve the best impact and to produce an empathetic grief counsellor.

These sessions are:

- Theory
- Practical

- Clinical session
- Town Hall Meeting

Over the years, the Foundation has worked with different partnersto make a tremendous impact on the life of traumatised Nigerians. They have included: MTN Nigeria, 7UP, Emzor Pharmaceutical Industries, the Murtala Muhammed Foundation, and the Chike Okoli Foundation.

Achievements

The Foundation has achieved tremendous success in the following:

- Installed traffic lights at the notorious Sobo Arobiodu/ Mobolaji Bank-Anthony intersection in Ikeja GRA. This move challenged the state government to put traffic lights all around the Lagos Metropolis
- In partnership with the Faculty of Behavioural Sciences ofLagos State University Teaching Hospital and under thestewardship of Professor Lambo, the first psychiatrist in Africa, evolved Aart of Life's pioneering four-step approach training in bereavement/trauma counselling
- We have subsequently maintained a very strong partnershipwith LASUTH, who have walked shoulder to shoulder withus during the evolution of Aart of Life Grief and Trauma Counselling, as we have acquired the formidable ground- breaking reputation we enjoy in Nigeria today

- Trained and certified three hundred and fifty grief and trauma counsellors (eighty more now selected for training).
- Established the first-ever grief and trauma counselling support service centre in Nigeria. Counselling was offeredfree of charge to Nigerians from all walks of life
- Produced a series of publications to support those experiencing trauma and grief, also to enlighten others on related issues
- Established in partnership with the MTN Nigeria Foundation, the 0703 Healing toll-free lines with trained counsellors, offering 24-hour grief/trauma counselling services
- The programme began in 2008 and ran for three years
- A partnership with Etisalat for the provision of fifteen toll-free lines was negotiated but faltered due to a crash in the GSM industry and associated restructuring and reduction in CSR initiatives
- The Aart of Life currently funds the toll-free grief and trauma counselling service directly, but without a sponsoring partner, advertising and demand is disappointingly limited
- Town hall meetings are an integral and important part of the Aart of Life grief and trauma training and they have been held every two years as the final part in the certificationof our counsellors
- Our first town hall meeting was in 2003 which was heldin the Aart of Life Training and Conference Centre witha remarkable group of four women who had lost their daughters. Our founder

was one of the women on the hot seat (as we call them) with an audience of about forty. A lot of healing always takes place at these events

- The Aart of Life Foundation took the initiative to design and run town hall grief counselling sessions following major disasters, including counselling parents of sixty children who died in the Port Harcourt Sosoliso Airline crash of 2005
- Initiated the 'Against all Odds' Awards, which evolved intothe innovative Against All Odds TV Docu-Drama. Two series of this gripping programme have so far been done in partnership with NTA and other electronic media. This further culminated in the 'Look at Me Now' Gala which was held in Lagos and the UK
- Created and lovingly maintained the Peaceful Gardens in the Ikeja GRA as a permanent memorial to Abioye AronkeTaiwo. To kick off the festive season every year, we switch on the Christmas lights at the Peaceful Gardens on 'Bioye'sbirthday, the 3rd of December
- In 2015, we organised an international symposium in Abuja titled "Setting an Agenda for the Future of Grief and Trauma Counselling in Nigeria"
- His Excellency, the Vice President, Professor Yemi Osinbajo, was a special guest of honour. The keynote address was delivered by the famous Professor David M. Ndetei of Nairobi University, Kenya, who had worked on a WHO-sponsored intervention in Kenya, following thegruesome attack by the Al-Shabaab terrorist group

- *Fear Abides with Me Constantly*, Abioye's book of poems beautifully edited by the ever so talented Toni Kan, was published in 2007, and reviewed by the celebrated writer, Dr Reuben Abati. The command performance as a dance drama by the talented Zara Udofia was presented on 19 April 2009, to rapturous reviews
- The dance drama has been promoted numerous times in Nigeria and always to rave and glowing reviews. Zara's famous dance troupe adapted some of the poems intoFrench, and gave a truly inspired performance during the Nigeria Creative Arts Exchange (NCAE) in May 2018, which was held in Pavillon Dauphine in Paris. This was a precursor event to President Macron's visit to Nigeria

0703 Healing: The MTN Nigeria Foundation Partnership Case Study

0703 Healing toll-free lines were established in partnership with the MTN Nigeria Foundation in 2008. Lines were manned by 75 trained counsellors offering 24-hour grief/trauma counselling services, mainly in the English language. The programme ran for three years.

The tele-counselling was fully sponsored by MTN, the African GSM giant. They supported us with two toll-free mobile phones anda landline and a sustained publicity programme to provide public awareness. This was the very first time such a programme had ever beenoffered in Nigeria.

It was an enormous success in spite of many constraints, for example: only two GSM lines and one landline and the calls were limitedto ten minutes per call. These constraints severely hampered the ability of our counsellors to effectively complete a session. We were obliged tocall back as they were routinely cut off after ten minutes, often as the sessions were reaching key unburdening and revelation point.

It undoubtedly provided a unique service to over 2,000 Nigeriansover the three years of operation, Nigerians who craved the anonymity this service offered. They were enabled to unburden emotions andtraumas they could not share with their closest family members, who were sometimes the source and cause of their angst.

Totally unexpected was the revelation that 70% of the callers were young men and that at least 70% of these young men came from the Northern States of Nigeria. Many of them exhibited an enormous amount of rage, rage against their societies and the situation in which they found themselves. We suspected that many of them were conflictedby their sexual orientation, a topic that was taboo in their society. We alsobelieve their frustrated and angry emotions and hopeless reality made them susceptible to joining terror organisations.

A few years later, when the Boko Haram terror attacks were unleashed in the Northern parts of Nigeria, we wondered, with great sadness, if any of our callers had joined the group, but hoped our services might have alleviated some of the great distress of those we had helped in the 0703 healing.

In April 2017, alarmed and disturbed by the wave of suicides all over Nigeria and across age and socio-economic groups, we initiated discussions, with the aim of developing a comprehensive programmeto address the specific problems and make available to the public our Aart

Of Life Counselling hotlines, in collaboration with our partners, psychiatrists and clinical psychologists of the School of Behavioural Sciences of LASUTH. Following a series of meetings between Lagos State Ministry of Health (LSMHT) led by Dr Dolapo Fasawe between 2017 and 2018, a partnership agreement was reached with LSMHT.

Subsequently, having developed selection criteria, graduates were selected through the Lagos State Employment Trust Fund (LSETF) and ArcSkills. These selection processes were managed by Aart of Life Foundation, ArcSkills, Vision to go and Princess Aderemi Adebowale.

Over the period of one week, graduates who met the criteriawere selected by a team of professionals. 80 graduates from LagosState Employment Trust Fund were shortlisted for a six-week training programme leading to the certification of the selected as Grief counsellors to be used in the call centre. The call centre is operational, but elections in 2019 and subsequent political instability delayed the progress of the grief and trauma counselling training of our selected 80 graduates. Our partners, the Lagos State Ministry of Health and Lagos State Government, remain fully committed to the scheme but are now consumed by the coronavirus pandemic; Lagos State, a megacity with apopulation of 20 million, is particularly vulnerable.

VISION 2038 AND ASPIRATIONS

Over our first eighteen years, Aart of Life Foundation has builta strong brand and reputation aligned to our core purposeto “promote and advance the virtues of love, kindness, compassion, charity, beauty, and sensitivity amongst all Nigerians, and especially amongst Abioye’s generation.”

We are proud of our achievements but realise what took us here, will not get us to the limitless vision future we desire. The emergenceof a ‘new normal’ created by the coronavirus pandemic of 2020, the coming ubiquity of 4G and smartphones in Nigeria, the likelihood of even higher incidence of prolonged grief disorder, the massive unmet needs for those suffering bereavement and trauma, a lack of psychiatristsand other trained mental health care professionals, and the inadequate response of government.

Our Board of Directors is currently undertaking a strategy reviewto reassess our Vision 2038—for our next eighteen years. We shall agreeon key pillars of our strategy (which will include grief and trauma counselling) and define the resources, capabilities and partnerships we must build to achieve our vision.

Within our work on grief, our aspiration includes taking our call centres and trauma and grief counselling centres national, supporting our compatriots all over Nigeria in their time of grief and trauma.

We also know that partnerships and leveraging mobile telephony are part of our distinctive competency and will remain so. We seek to partner with international organisations, to leverage technology to offer apps downloadable to smartphones. Today there are estimated to be 25 to40 million smartphone users in Nigeria, a figure projected to increase to140 million by 2025. We seek to broaden our reach to distressed Nigerians by offering support to the chronically bereaved and distressed, and thosewho support them, with innovative tools offered through smartphones.

The directors of the Foundation comprise of the following members:

- Chief Mrs Taiwo Taiwo (Chairman)
- Dr Mrs Stella Okoli OON
- Mrs Joke Jacobs MFR
- Mrs Pamela Watson
- Professor Bolanle Ola
- Mr Ladipo Taiwo
- Mr Leye Taiwo

Aart of Life Foundation is managed by an excellent management team, under the direction of the Chairman/Founder, Taiwo Taiwo, who drivesmany of the initiatives with the innate passion and devotion with which she puts into all things Aart of Life. She is supported by the executive secretary, Aisha Eliakwu; a team of executives; and a number of volunteers; all of whom manage the counsellors.

TRIBUTE TO MY BELOVED MOTHER

Written on the 25th of April, 2006, the day of her passing

There was a pause, just long enough for an angel topass, flying slowly.

— Ronald Firbank

My mother, an icon of uncommon motherly love.

My extraordinary mother Alice Olaperi Shonibare (née Olukoya), was born on the 16th of March, 1923, the first born of Samuel Ademola Olukoya, and his wife, Jolade Olukoya (née Idowu). Both her parents were of the Ruling Houses of Odogbolu, Ijebu; her father, Samuel Ademola Olukoya, of the Oremadegun Ruling House, her mother, of the Ajeloreawo Ruling House. Her maternal grandfather, Oba Ajeloreawo, was renowned for his great wealth and wisdom. Her parents' church wedding was a grand affair.

She was raised in a rarefied and prosperous home by her Sierra Leonean-trained seamstress mother and her CMS Grammar School-educated father who rose to become (together with Mr Solanke) one of the first African Managers of UAC.

Her father worked and lived extensively in various regions of the Old Western Region (Ilesha, Owo, Akure) returning home to Ijebu Ode on his retirement, to become one of the most successful businessmen ofthe region. She was nevertheless brought up to be extremely humble, modest and self-effacing.

She was the only child of her parents for many years, until her younger brother, Dewole, arrived thirteen years later.

Four years after that, the first tragedy that defined who she was occurred. Her beloved mother aged thirty-four years, died suddenly, followed closely by her grandmother who, heartbroken by the loss of her only child, died six months later. Leaving my mother, at age fourteen, mother to her younger brother, Dewole.

Her life would thereafter be defined by her extraordinary capacityas a loving mother.

She was educated at UMS Ibadan, studying Domestic Science after, but she had already acquired her intuitive entrepreneurial spirit.

With the approval of her father she married, in August 1946, young Suleiman Olatunbosun Shonibare, who was then working under her father at UAC. Her father consented to the marriage on condition that he change his religion and become a Christian.

Suleiman Olatunbosun Shonibare became Samuel Olatunbosun Shonibare. They had one of the grandest weddings Ijebu Ode has ever seen.

Her marriage was remarkable not only for the love, but for the uncommon partnership she and her husband shared in their endeavours.

Her husband was an exceptionally forward-looking young man, way ahead of his generation. He grew to be an innovative and astute businessman, a politician with a true sense of social justice, renowned for his generosity. Together, they were formidable.

When her husband died in 1964 aged forty-four, leaving her at theage of forty-one, a widow with eight children—the eldest of whom was seventeen years old, and the youngest, four—the second great tragedy that defined her life occurred. Her exceptional character shone through it;her will of steel, her ability to analyse issues and forge the right solutions,her humility, but most importantly, exceptional love for her children.

She dealt with insurmountable problems from various businesses of her companies, dealt with so many financial crises, treachery, problems with teenage children who had been educated expensively in the UK, and angst of settling termly fees. She told stories of receiving school bills from some of the schools, and not knowing how she was going to deal with them, bargaining for more time by writing the school, requesting forthe school bill already in hand!

Her children always came first, bar nothing. She would drop anything, cancel any appointment, including a visit to BuckinghamPalace to meet the Queen, if a child of hers had a problem anywherein the world—this actually happened. But she would not hesitate to discipline her children firmly and decisively if needed. She taught us values, a sense of commitment and purpose. It is not an accident thatall her eight children graduated with a minimum of a first degree, that amongst them were doctors, lawyers, accountants, etc., this was the minimum expectation she demanded.

She was an astute businesswoman, forward-looking and intuitive,but because of her self-effacing and humble personality, she simply wasnot interested in singing the amazing successes she personally recorded, turning around the company, Shonny Investments & Properties Company Limited, with the myriad problems it faced following the death of her husband: the creation of the Maryland Guest House, which later became the very successful Maryland Hotel, out of the children's wing of our home; acquiring Elephant House and the plots surrounding it, building the eighteen-storey Elephant House in Lagos.

In 1993, in another demonstration of her love for her children, shedid something exceptional, without precedence. She divided the assets ofher company equally among her eight children, prayed for all of them, and gave them her blessings with their future endeavours.

It is a measure of the exceptional nature of this remarkable icon, that even though the only asset she kept for herself, the eighteen-storey Elephant House situated on Broad Street, almost immediately following her remarkable generosity suffered a devastating and unexpected decline arising from the collapse of Lagos Island, she never contemplated changing the post.

A fashion icon, she had elegance, grace, and a sense of fun.

With an amazing sense of humour, ever the politician's wife, she loved nothing better than joining in a hearty political discussion, whetherit be Nigerian politics, British, or American; she was a much-loved mother, grandmother, aunty, sister, and mentor of many. Her home was always welcoming, always filled with those who loved her, loved her company, and was always filled with vitality.

A devoted Christian, she was for many years a pillar of St Paul's Church, Breadfruit, until the founding of the Archbishop Vining Memorial Church, Ikeja. She was revered in these churches as a member of the Band of Grace Society. She served as Matron of the Cathedral Beacon Society of Our Saviour's Church, Ijebu Ode. She went to Holy Communion every day until when the aches and pain of her final years prevented her.

She had an undying love and respect for her husband. And even though he died forty-four years before her, hardly a day went by that she did not recall him with love.

My darling mother, My Icon, My Anchor, My Pillar, My Strength, when you crossed over majestically surrounded by your loved ones, with the vicar saying the communion that Tuesday morning, the heaven opened up to welcome you home triumphantly, led by your beloved husband and granddaughter, 'Bioye, and it must have been a glorious day in heaven. But what a sad day for us your beloved ones here on earthto lose such an exceptional, extraordinary Mother.

We give glory to the Almighty for your extraordinary life and for bringing us to your fold.

Dear Reader,

My Mother's Daughter started as a homage to my mother. I had this compelling need to tell her story, and as I proceeded, it became clear that in so doing, so very much of my life was inextricably linked to her.I could not have achieved or even dared to embark on so many of the gutsy initiatives I have throughout my adult life, if I had not had such a formidable role model as my mother.

In telling my story, *My Mother's Daughter*, I discovered that she hadled me on my journey to becoming.

But there was more. Having learnt so early in life, the truism of those words of Mahatma Ghandi's so famously paraphrased, *be the change you wish to see in the world*, I believed I had a special duty to impart onothers, and especially the next generation, the importance of pressure groups as a means of forcing change in our society. Margaret Mead wasso right when she said that it is not whether pressure groups can change the world. The fact is it is the only thing that ever has.

So many people, too many, moan and groan about issues they feelso passionately about, but seem paralysed as to how to go about doing something about it.

I hope that by showing—through my life's varied experiences as a social entrepreneur—and demonstrating the process I have adoptedon multiple occasions in setting up successful pressure groups, achievingan obligatory critical mass of people who share the passion, and most importantly, agreeing on strategic immediate-, medium- and long-term visions, it can be a spring board to force the change we desire.

Do not forget to celebrate the small victories which will empowerand propel you to bigger ones, and ultimately, we will achieve the tremendous changes we all so badly desire in our society.

This time-tested formula was how Atlantic Hall, LIMGE, Aart of Life, were initiated and evolved to become such powerful change agents.

My overarching message to you is this, STOP getting angry and frustrated with things that truly grate you and your sensibilities, organisea pressure group around your passion, be tenacious, and be prepared to stay the course. You too can change our world, and we can all aspire to live in the Nigeria of our dreams.

We deserve to. God knows we do.

Sincerely,

Taiwo Taiwo

Acknowledgements

An important life lesson I have wholeheartedly embraced is that every one of us is gifted with multiple talents that lie dormant, untapped, within us.It is, quite frankly, sinful not to explore as many of our God-given talentsas possible, while we are living and breathing.

I thank God for the privilege to have had a mother who encouragedme to explore each one of these talents.

The greatest threat to realising our full potential is procrastination.

It paralyses many from pursuing a rich, creative and fulfilling life.

I have also learnt that you don't have to be born in the same mother's womb to find your true siblings.

I consider one of my greatest fortunes being blessed with suchan amazing sister as Dr Stella Okoli, Founder and Managing Directorof Emzor Pharmaceutical. She is certainly someone who has used the multiple talents God has endowed her with.

She recently completed the multi-billion-dollar World Health Organisation-approved pharmaceutical factory where her hundreds of products are already being exported to Europe and beyond. A loving friend who will never allow you feel down when life throws you the occasional curveball, she is always there in a jiffy to stand shoulder-to-shoulder with me, sharing in my joy, an incomparable shoulder to lean on in my moments of sorrow, generous to a fault.

My sweetheart, Joke Jacobs. My darling younger sister. We can chat, and we do chat, about everything and anything.

My oyinbo besto, Pamela Watson, and her husband, a real treasureof a friend.

My childhood sister and friend, Eniola Fadayomi.

It's amazing, but come to think of it, my special bond with many of these special sisters God brought to me all came following the passingof my dearest darling, 'Bioye.

My daughters, 'Bioye's dearest friends, who made sure even with a table with a missing spot for 'Bioye in our household, they were there to fill the gap. I was the mother of the bride at each one of their weddings. Angella Nwadion Eseka, Ndidi Nwuneli, and Elke Bull, my German daughter. So many daughters gained on earth when my one and only daughter, 'Bioye, departed so suddenly.

Debo Dina Adebayo, my darling niece.

My sons, Ladipo and his wife, Yemisi; Leye; and the grandchildren they have brought into my life to love and cherish.

Ladi, my husband, knowing exactly when I needed him most, holding me tight and never letting go.

A book that prepared me for so much of life's surprising twists and turns was given to me by my late friend, Nikue Akpe, *Necessary Losses*by Judith Viorst. What an incredible book. It prepared me, long before

I knew what lay in front of me, for the loves, illusions, dependencies and impossible expectations that all of us have. Everyone must read this amazing book at least once in their lifetime.

The overarching message of *My Mother's Daughter* however is perfectly encapsulated in this passage from *A Return to Love* by Marianne Williamson:

> *Our deepest fear is not that we are inadequate, our deepest fearis that we are powerful beyond measure.*
>
> *It is our light, not our darkness that most frightens us. We ask ourselves, 'Who am I to be brilliant, gorgeous, talented, and fabulous?' Actually, who are you not to be? You are a childof God. Your playing small does not serve the world. There is nothing enlightened about shrinking so other people won't feel insecure around you. We are all meant to shine, as children do. We were born to manifest the glory of God that is within us. It's not just in some of us, it's in everyone. And as we let our own light shine, we unconsciously give other people permission to do the same. As we are liberated from our own fear, our presenceautomatically liberates others.*

About the Author

Chief Mrs Taiwo Taiwo is the Chairman, Lexham Investment—owners of Shonny Investment and Properties Company (SIPC) Ltd. She has overforty-five years' experience in the real estate industry as a developer both in and outside Nigeria, covering the commercial and residential markets.

At age 28, she was appointed Director of Operations at Shonny Investment and Properties Co. Ltd., and was given the responsibility of arranging the financing of the Elephant House project, an eighteen- storey development on Broad Street, Lagos. She had direct responsibility for coordinating the finance and paying back the bridge and debenture loans which she completed, making Shonny Investment and Properties Company Ltd. the first company to have discharged its obligation as and when due in the history of the Nigerian capital marketing. She was 32 years.

Chief Taiwo is the founding and current Chairman of the acclaimed secondary school, Atlantic Hall, a co-educational non-profit secondary school.

She is founding Chairman and Trustee of Lagos MillenniumGroup on the Environment (LIMGE)—a non-profit pressure group of business leaders, stakeholders, and concerned citizens of Lagos, working to arrest the deterioration of infrastructure in Lagos, improve the environment, and make Lagos the 'Venice of Africa'. Under her leadership, an ultra-modern fire station, the Ajele Fire Station—with funds donated by Shell—was built, equipped to the highest standard in the world, and donated to the Lagos State Government for the benefit of the Lagos Island community.

Chief Taiwo is a committed social entrepreneur. Over the years, she has sat on the board of Fate Foundation as a founding member. She sits on the board of the Chike Okoli Foundation.

In August 2002, following the death of her 24-year-old daughter four months earlier, she founded the Aart of Life Foundation, inspired by the life of her daughter, Abioye Aronke Taiwo, and an acronym of her name. The foundation was established to promote and advance the virtues of love, compassion, charity, and beauty, amongst all Nigerians. The foundation has pioneered grief and trauma counselling in Nigeria, working with multiple local and international organisations, and has recently partnered with the Lagos State Government to train carefully selected graduate counsellors for a 24-hour call centre pilot scheme.

On the 17th of July, 2019, Chief Mrs Taiwo Taiwo was givenan honorary award by the Chartered Institute of Public Resources Management & Politics in Ghana, for her outstanding, trailblazing entrepreneurship achievement in Africa.

www.ingramcontent.com/pod-product-compliance
Ingram Content Group UK Ltd.
Pitfield, Milton Keynes, MK11 3LW, UK
UKHW062303290726
14090UKWH00017B/853

9 789785 849455